HARDEST GEEZER

HARDEST GEEZER

MIND OVER MILES

RUSS COOK

flightbooks

1

Flight Books, part of Flight Studio, a Flight Group company

In collaboration with Ebury Spotlight, an imprint of Ebury Publishing
Penguin Random House UK
One Embassy Gardens, 8 Viaduct Gardens,
Nine Elms, London SW11 7BW

Ebury Publishing is part of the Penguin Random House group of companies
whose addresses can be found at global.penguinrandomhouse.com

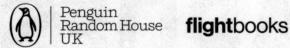

First published by Flight Books in 2024

www.flightbooks.com
www.penguin.co.uk

A CIP catalogue record for this book is available from the British Library

Hardback ISBN 9781529945928
Trade Paperback ISBN 9781529950038

Printed and bound in Australia by Griffin Press

The authorised representative in the EEA is Penguin Random House Ireland,
Morrison Chambers, 32 Nassau Street, Dublin D02 YH68.

Penguin Random House is committed to a sustainable future
for our business, our readers and our planet. This book is
made from Forest Stewardship Council® certified paper.

I dedicate this book to my mum and dad.
I know I didn't make life easy for you, but you gave me
the strength and independence to become who I am today.
I'll always be grateful for everything you've done.

'A journey of a thousand miles begins with a single step.'

— Laozi, *Dao De Jing*

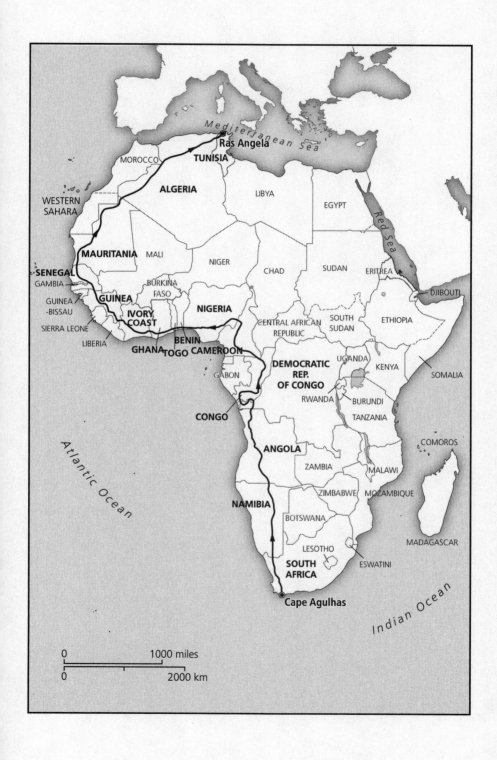

CONTENTS

PROLOGUE

I'm the third man on the back of a bike built for one. There's nowhere to rest my feet. I'm cramped and tense. Sweating and dirty.

Sick with fear.

On either side of me lies thick, impenetrable rainforest. Behind me lies a narrow, winding jungle path. Ahead of me? Who knows? I don't know where they're taking me. I don't know what they intend.

All I know is that these two men are not my friends. I'm not on this bike willingly. Truth is, I don't have a choice.

Already today I've pounded 50 kilometres of hard jungle road. I've escaped men with machetes, then hidden in the jungle while they circled me. I'm weak with dehydration and hunger. I've lost my friends. I've lost my sense of direction.

I've lost any hope that I'm going to get out of this in one piece.

I truly think I'm going to die.

As I grip the body of that juddering motorbike, I can't help but think how stupid I've been. I can't help but think that I've let everybody down. I left England without properly fixing things with my mum and dad, and there was plenty that needed fixing. I imagine them receiving the news that I've gone missing. I imagine the intolerable worry and stress.

I picture them at home, weeks from now, hearing that my body has finally been found.

I wish I could speak to them, just once. I wish I could tell them that I regretted the way I'd handled things when I was younger.

I wish I could tell them that I was sorry.

I wish I could tell them that I loved them.

I'd always meant to. I'd always thought that, at some point, I'd reach out to my family and make amends for my mistakes. I think of those mistakes now, as the motorbike trundles over stony ground further into the darkness, and the voices of my captors become increasingly hostile.

Just over a hundred days ago, I set out from the southern tip of Africa. My mission: to run the entire length of the continent. Plenty of people told me it was madness. They told me it couldn't be done. They told me I'd die.

Looks like they were right.

So now, with my fate in the hands of my two aggressive captors, I blink away the tears, close my eyes and think of home.

I think of family.

I think of loved ones.

I think of all the paths I've gone down to lead me to this point …

1

TEENAGE GEEZER

My paternal granddad was not one to follow the rules. My maternal granddad was a man of discipline and structure. I see myself in both of them, and both of them in myself.

My paternal granddad was born in 1944 and never knew his own dad, an American airman who found himself in the south of England during the Second World War. His mum brought him up on her own. Money was scarce and as a teenager he frequently found himself in trouble with the police. It was petty stuff – driving motorbikes around his hometown of Shoreham-by-Sea without insurance, getting into fights, running away from police, doing the usual kind of things that a certain type of teenager does. As a young man he took an apprenticeship as an engineer, but it didn't pay much money so he also worked as a bouncer in a Brighton club. It was here that he met my nan. They married quickly and within a year my dad was born. My grandparents stayed married for 18 years, but my granddad was not a man who found satisfaction in the day-to-day of a normal life and so the marriage broke down. He then travelled the world, wandering through Australia and Asia, entering and leaving a string of relationships, until he finally met and married a Thai woman in 2004.

They returned to the UK, but even with his wandering days behind him, his distaste for the rules remained. Even now he's always in trouble with someone about something. He doesn't want to be told what to do. Eight years ago, he was diagnosed with terminal cancer and given a year to live. Even the disease couldn't control him. He ignored the doctors' instructions to stop drinking and maxed out his credit cards so that he had enough money to enjoy the life that was left.

Despite his rogue decisions that might be questionable to some, my grandad is also a very lovable man and very loving himself. I've never seen him so distraught as when remembering his dogs who have died. My granddad has taught me that it's possible to be big-hearted and stubborn at the same time.

My maternal granddad, who lives 600 miles away, has been less present in my life. He joined the RAF at a young age and remained in the service until he retired as a warrant officer, the top rank an NCO can achieve. His job required him to travel when my mum was young – Gibraltar, Germany, Wales – before finally settling down in his hometown of Forres in Scotland. He was old school: traditional, disciplined and well respected. He was a military man who excelled in sports. He was a fast runner and good at football.

When I was 15 years old, my parents sent me to stay with him in the wilds of Scotland for a summer. I'd been misbehaving. I guess they needed some respite, and they felt that my disciplinarian granddad would be a good influence on me. I didn't want to go. Like most 15-year-olds I wanted to be going to parties and drinking with my mates down the park. None of that was happening in this little Scottish town.

One day he announced that we were going on a long bike ride. My nan presented us with a packed lunch of tuna sandwiches. I didn't really like tuna, and I said so. Another grandparent might have mollycoddled me. No chance. It was tuna sandwiches or nothing. And it was a long ride through the woods or nothing. My granddad was a serious guy and I didn't complain. Something about him inspired respect. I responded to his discipline.

Which was unusual, because the young Russ Cook was extremely bad at doing what he was told.

• • •

I was a bright enough boy when I was very young, and good at school. My end-of-year reports from the Vale Primary School in West Sussex were generally very positive. I had lots of friends. I lived for football; I played it at school, at weekends and at after-school training sessions. In fact, I played football four or five times a week until the age of 16. Being part of a team with my friends gave me some of my best childhood memories. My parents did a great job of facilitating my passion for football and sport. David Beckham was my idol and I dreamed of being a professional footballer like him. Maybe it could happen? After all, I was captain of the school team and played for Worthing United. Being small, fast and left-footed I started out on the wing before moving into the centre – but although I was a decent enough little player, I was never good enough to be the next Becks. My dream of being a pro player would remain just that: a dream.

Still, I was athletic and energetic and whenever I was out and about with my dad, he'd give me little challenges. 'Run to the lamp-post and back and I'll give you 10 pence.' 'Run up that hill and I'll give you 20 pence.' I suppose I was motivated in part by the pocket money. Really, though, it was my dad's good opinion that mattered to me. I wanted to impress him. I wanted him to be proud of my little achievements.

My dad was a tool grinder. He bought my grandad's old tools and set up a workshop. It was a dark, grimy, industrial place stinking of metal and sweat. Dad would come home from work covered in metal dust. I don't remember seeing much of him in those days, but I remember looking at how big and strong he was. Grinding tools was hard, relentless work. My dad was good at it and he took his role as a provider for the family very seriously. I knew, though, even as a small kid, that I didn't want that to be my future. My mother was a full-time mum alongside working part-time jobs and she was amazing. She was nurturing, attentive and very organised, but she had her hands full with three boister-ous boys. And she had her hands full with other things too.

One Christmas Eve, our fairly normal family life was ruptured. Suddenly, my dad, without any warning or reason, started to behave strangely. He called several ambulances, telling them that people were coming to get us. He stalked round the house turning off anything electrical, including the TV and radio, because he thought mysterious figures were trying to contact us. This sudden psychosis meant he had to be sectioned. It predictably led to strains in the household. And I knew that my dad's behaviour had changed somewhat, now that he was on heavy medication for his mental health issues.

It affected me. I would wake up in the middle of the night, crying. I lacked the tools to process what was going on around me in a healthy way. This was before conversations about mental health were open and widespread in society, as they are today. I didn't know what to do with these feelings, so I did nothing with them. I kept them inside. In my young mind I decided on some level that I should not allow myself to linger around these emotions. I needed to move on. I didn't understand that negative emotions, left unprocessed, often appear in different and unwelcome manifestations later on.

My brother Ben is ten months older than me, my brother Andy is nearly two years younger. We got on well as kids, and I have lots of great memories of us together. Some highlights include playing indoor football in the lounge (my mum was never a fan of this one) or the floor is lava, and making dens in the woods.

We also had the usual brotherly fights pretty frequently, and as we got older, they got more and more real, particularly between me and my older brother. When I was 14, we fell out very badly. I was very spiteful and hateful towards my brother at that age and in retrospect, it was the beginning of me withdrawing from my family.

The transition into adolescence is a difficult one for most young people. In many respects I was no different to anybody else my age. As my freedom increased, my responsibilities grew. I gained more independence from my family, which I appreciated, but I also had to choose my GCSEs and, like many teenagers, I felt the foreboding of an unknown future. I looked at my mum and dad and didn't see people living a life I wanted to live. That realisation had a profound effect on me. This made me feel reluctant to listen to anything they had to say.

It is not unusual for a child to clash with his or her parents as they negotiate adolescence. My behaviour, though, was extreme. I feel ashamed, now I look back through the lens of adulthood. My parents' expectations were not unreasonable. They wanted me to speak politely to them. They wanted me to treat the house, and the family, with a basic level of respect. The 14-year-old me failed to understand the importance of this. All I heard was instructions rather than explanations. I saw no reason to follow rules that I didn't understand. Maybe it was a trait I inherited from my paternal granddad. Maybe it was all my own doing. Either way, it led me down a difficult path. When my mum told me that I had to be home by a certain time, I'd ignore her and come back whenever I wanted to. If they left the house for a few days, I would throw big parties and trash the whole place. I guess none of these behaviours were particularly unusual in isolation, but cumulatively, they developed into a lack of respect on my part for my parents that eventually led to the complete breakdown of the relationship.

At school, I was placed in the gifted and talented set and was expected to do really well. However, my GCSE courses coincided with this change in my behaviour and my academic performance soon deteriorated. I told myself I didn't care. Exams seemed to me to be an integral part of a system that insisted I had to follow a particular path if I wanted to succeed. Pass this exam to get this job. Get this job to have a nice life. The system held no attraction for me. I didn't want to be constrained by its rules. I felt quite certain I could fail at everything everybody told me I *had* to do, and still enjoy my life. What the hell did anybody else know? I wanted to prove people wrong simply for the sake of proving people wrong.

I feel conflicted when I remember my teenage self. The path I chose back then turned out okay for me in the end, but I'm well aware that I was very fortunate to turn into this version of myself; it would have been all too easy for me to have followed a self-destructive path and turned into someone completely different. And I very nearly did.

I may not have been interested in the approval of my parents any more, but I was very interested in the approval of my peers. I just wanted to be one of the boys. Football became more about partying with my teammates than about the game itself. I craved their validation. I wanted to wear the same clothes, have the same hairstyle, hang out at the same parties. And I wanted no involvement from my parents because I felt that they were an obstacle to the way I wanted to live my life. My mum would ask me perfectly normal questions – 'Will you be home for dinner?' 'Can you join us for a family event at the weekend?' My response would not be that of a normal human being: I would give rude one-word answers. I said horrible things when she pointed out that I was living under her roof. I'd tell her it wasn't hers, it was Dad's, because he was the one that paid for it all. I would be purposely divisive and sabotage things to emphasise how much I felt our family sucked. And if, of all things, my parents presumed to offer me any advice, my response would be particularly contemptuous and savage. It embarrasses me to recall the things I said. 'Why would I take your advice? You've never done anything with your life. Shut your mouth.'

I can't imagine how hard it was for my parents to receive this relentless barrage of brutal insults and dismissiveness. What I do know is that their natural response was to fight the fire of my disdain with the fire of their own anger and outrage. My unpleasant responses triggered vicious arguments. 'We've never done anything with our life? You've never done anything with yours, and you never will.' No doubt my parents felt so heavily disrespected that they thought it necessary to humble me in some way. With hindsight I can understand their reaction. At the time, these comments only bolstered my determination that I needed nobody else to help me find my way in life, least of all them. I wouldn't let them make me feel like I was never going to do anything in my life. I became filled with resentment and fury, but also with a determination that I would show them how wrong they were if they thought I couldn't live life on my own.

And so, at the age of 17, while I was still at college doing my A-levels, when the arguments had become too savage and the mutual resentment too difficult for any of us to live with, I moved out.

2

GAMBLING GEEZER

It was a traumatic time for us all. In my head I had framed the situation as me versus them, but they weren't monsters. They didn't want to see me crash and burn. My presence had just become too much for my family to bear.

When I was out of the house one day, my parents moved my stuff over to my granddad's and locked me out. I recovered my things and returned home. I remember creeping round to the back of the house when it was dark outside and looking in through the window to see my dad standing in the kitchen. A mad rage boiled inside me – rage that I now see had been my constant companion since my early teens – and I head-butted the window. The glass didn't shatter but my dad looked terrified. It's not a good feeling to have your dad stare at you in that way. I think I knew then that they really meant it when they said I couldn't live under their roof any more.

I remember feeling terribly betrayed by this turn of events but determined that I would prove my parents wrong. They thought I couldn't live alone? They thought they could humble me by stamping out my desire to live my life the way I wanted? Bring it on. I would show them, and everyone, that I was completely self-reliant.

I walked into an estate agent and said, 'I need a flat.' The cheapest available was £425 a month. I said, 'I'll take it.'

But now I needed money.

I didn't claim any benefits. I was too proud for all of that. My parents and grandparents had contributed to a small fund since I was born. We found ourselves in a complicated situation, but deep down they wanted the best for me so they gave me this money when I moved out. It helped set me up with the basics but once it was spent I had no other income.

I was not afraid of hard work, however. From my paternal granddad I'd learned a disrespect for the rules, but from my maternal granddad I'd learned an ability to graft. At the age of 12, I had a paper round. At 15, I took a weekend job in a café. At 16, I started doing cleaning jobs. I would get up a 4.30 in the morning to clean at the local supermarket. I had another cleaning job in the evening after school. When it became apparent that I really was going to have to back up my words with actions and earn my own money if I wanted to prove my self-reliance to my parents and to the world, I started a little business cleaning people's houses. I printed out flyers, which I distributed through letterboxes and behind windscreen wipers. My attendance at college plummeted to well under 50 per cent so that I could earn enough to make my rent. I was always skint. Many was the time that I presented my card at Lidl and whispered a silent prayer that it would work. It often didn't.

I was proper excited when I received the keys and first walked into that tiny one-bedroom flat. Inwardly, I was daunted. I'd made such a big deal in front of my parents of my ability to be auton-omous, and I now had to prove myself. My flat became a party place at the weekends, but during the week I had to work my cleaning jobs as much as possible while attending college as often as I could. For a while my motivation not to return home sheep-ishly gave me the energy I needed. The time came, however, when things started to slip.

I finished college. Now that I was free to start a full-time job, I decided I wanted to try my hand at sales. It struck me as being the best-paying job that required no experience or qualifications. I took a position in recruitment sales. I soon realised, in that provincial *Wolf of Wall Street* environment, that the way to please your boss was to have the phone constantly to your ear. I would make 150 calls a day, and for a while I quite enjoyed the novelty of that work-hard-play-hard vibe.

The novelty, however, soon wore off. It was a dog-eat-dog world. Nobody had any friends. Everybody was out for themselves. And it was relentless. I'd wake up early, rush to work and make cold calls for 12 or 13 hours. Back home, I'd collapse, exhausted, eat some shit food, fall asleep and repeat the same process the next day and the next. I grew to hate it: the repetitive grind, the sense that I was doing nothing with my life despite my grand claims to my parents.

I found relief from the monotony of my daily life in two pursuits. One was drinking. Come the weekend, I'd binge drink with my friends, throwing beer down my neck as a way of forgetting about the drudgery of my day job. My Fridays, Saturdays and Sundays were routinely lost at the bottom of a bottle.

The other pursuit, which I thought offered me a way out but which only trapped me further, was gambling.

. . .

I first started gambling at the age of 15 when I was still living with my parents. It was nothing serious, at least it didn't seem so at the time. Just the occasional flutter on football accumulators, back when the restrictions on young people gambling were not so strict and the pursuit seemed like nothing more than an extension of my enthusiasm for the game. A little bet on the Champions League? An opportunity to put your money where your mouth was if you thought United would have a big night? It was all part of the football culture with which I identified. I had hardly any money to gamble at the time – really no more than my paper-round money – and even if I lost it all, the consequences were not severe. I still had a roof over my head, and food on the table.

When I moved out of my parents' house, and I was working every hour I could just to pay my way, it continued to be a fun diversion. By the time I was 19, however, with a full-time income and the growing suspicion that my career was not turning out the way I wanted it to, gambling became a bigger part of my life.

Addictions don't happen overnight. They arrive gradually. They sneak up on you when you're not looking. I was not aware, as I tried to replicate the buzz of winning £30 on the football, that anything untoward was taking place when I decided to have a little go at online roulette. It was just a way of relaxing. A fun way to pass the time. And if I won a few quid, so much the better.

I thought I was being sensible, to begin with. I'd sit down of an evening and tell myself that I wouldn't bet more than £20 on the roulette. When that was gone, I'd call it a night. From time to time, I'd be up. Mostly I'd be down. That's the way it works. But I kept a check on my spending and it wasn't a problem.

Until it was.

I'd tell myself that, having lost £20 the previous night, I'd check out this evening when I was *up* £20. And I seldom was, so the £20 became £40, the £40 became £50 and the £50 became £100.

And then I was betting a grand a night.

And then I was betting my entire pay packet.

And then I was maxing out my credit cards, and using up my bank overdraft, betting with money I didn't have and couldn't afford.

We delude ourselves easily. I was certainly delusional then. I didn't see myself as a kid sitting alone in his flat, throwing his money away and running up debts I could never afford to pay off. I saw myself as a smart guy with a strategy to make a ton of cash. I saw myself as the one who would make the betting companies take a hit. Even though I might encounter the occasional bump in the road, my strategy would come good if I just stuck to the plan. My debts didn't make me miserable. They were just the inevitable consequences of the struggle I had to overcome. They were the cost of doing business.

I admitted to nobody what was happening. Occasionally I would discuss bets with my friends who still wagered on the footy. If I'd won, I'd tell them. I never disclosed my losses. I wanted to present the persona of a winner, not a loser.

But everyone who gambles is a loser in the end.

I was certainly losing, and not just financially. I hated my job. It took up so many hours of my day and gave me nothing in return, other than the money I needed to sustain my gambling habit. I lived on a terrible diet of frozen food, takeaways, sausage rolls and pizza. All my favourite things to eat, but it did nothing for my health or state of mind. I became quite overweight. Physically, I'd not yet developed into a man. I still had the frame of a little boy. There was no muscle on me and I was not yet able to grow a beard. My lifestyle barely required me to move. I did no exercise at all so I started to pile a fair bit of fat onto that skinny frame.

I don't know if it was the lack of exercise that made my mood drop, or if I stopped exercising because of my low mood. All I know is that I'd gone from being the kid at school who'd been voted sportsman of the year, who was captain of the football team and a keen cross-country runner, to becoming a sedentary, unhealthy 19-year-old. I was struggling badly. I had lots of friends but I couldn't admit this drop in my mood to anybody. I couldn't even admit it to myself. So even when I woke up at night crying, just like I had done as a kid, I lacked the tools to make sense of what was happening. I didn't know how to acknowledge my feelings. I didn't know how to name the beast. Pretty much all my time outside of work was taken up with gambling or partying. I became caught up in a culture of binge drinking, so while I wasn't drinking every night, when I *did* drink I really went for it. It wasn't fun. I felt trapped. Suffocated. In retrospect I suppose this was an exaggerated version of the suffocation I'd felt throughout my teenage years. Now, though, I had nobody to blame but myself. I was in charge of my life, and I wasn't making a good job of it.

I was in a club in Worthing one night when I got really pissed. One of my mates got into an argument. Everything became a bit heated and I tussled with some other lads. The rage that I'd always carried inside me burst out and I really started kicking off. The bouncers chucked me out of the club and I gave them a bit of aggro. The police came, arrested me and chucked me into the back of the van. I thought they were going to give me a lift home. In fact, they gave me a lift to the police station. I carried on mouthing off unpleasantly to everyone in the station, so they put me in a cell for the night. I woke up the next morning aching all over, with a splitting head and a crushing sense of embarrassment at my drunken behaviour the previous night. They gave me a fine, a slap on the wrist and sent me home.

It wasn't my only run-in with the police. I might have stopped playing football, but my mates and I sometimes went to watch games. My mates and I were bored at a football match and started betting each other that we wouldn't dare run onto the pitch. I took that dare. The police arrested me and I was banned from Portsmouth football club for life. At the station I mouthed off again at anyone who'd listen, trying to goad the officers into punching me. 'You're all losers! You're just policemen! You've got no money! What are you going to do, be a copper all your life?' It was the most terrible behaviour. It shames me to recall it. My words were ironic, of course, because *I* was the loser with no money. *I* was the one whose life was heading nowhere. Yet again

I was finding someone else to blame for everything that I was doing wrong.

I had a girlfriend at the time. She was good to me, but I wasn't in the right headspace to return her affection and kindness. My life was consumed by work, binge drinking, aggressive behaviour and, of course, online roulette. My debts became so extreme that I found myself lying to her. I said that my boss had failed to pay my commission, so I didn't have enough money for the rent. The second bit was true enough. Not the first. I'd spent everything and exhausted every line of credit available to me. My gambling habit had completely consumed me. It had ceased to be a fun way to pass the time and become a terrible burden. I suddenly realised how deluded I'd been. I was not the smart guy with a clever scheme to make a million. I was just another victim of the gambling industry. I'd messed up, big time.

If I didn't do something about it, I couldn't even guess how bad things might become.

3

MARATHON GEEZER

More than anything else, it was embarrassment at what my life had turned into that made me quit gambling. I didn't want to be that guy, the guy who lied to his girlfriend about why he needed to borrow money. The addiction had crept on me so slowly that for a long while I didn't realise how bad it had become. Lying to my girlfriend made me check myself. It made me take an objective look at what I was doing with my life, and I didn't like what I saw.

I banned myself from every gambling website. Many people, when they're in as deep as I was, find it difficult to go cold turkey. I'm grateful that I found the strength from somewhere. I knew, though, that quitting the gambling was only a first step. I was still deeply immersed in lad culture, which can be fun but also very toxic. So often it's an evolution of that teenage peer pressure where anything you do outside of the norm of the tribe is heavily scrutinised and criticised. As a teenager, if you roll into school with a different haircut to everyone else, you get roasted for it. Similarly, as a young man, your contemporaries can sometimes be critical if you don't do what's expected of you. You're not coming to the pub tonight? You're not drinking? Loser!

I felt the influence of my peers deeply. No doubt I wasn't the only one. I think we were crabs in a bucket, trying to escape but pulling each other down, and I was one of the biggest crabs. So, although I had managed to kick the gambling, I was still binge drinking, eating shit food, failing to exercise and letting the lairy side of my nature occasionally get the better of me. In this, I was not so different from my friends, or I suppose from many other young men, unsure of themselves and how to express their masculinity.

What does it mean to be a young man in a world where there is so much mixed messaging around masculinity? I didn't know, at the time. I didn't want to express my masculinity in a toxic way, but at some level I did want to express it. Hard, when you have a shit job, when you're skint, when your prospects are poor and you're not much of a catch for any young women. By now my girlfriend and I had broken up and I was on the lookout for a new girlfriend, but I found the dating scene confusing. Some girls seemed to want a dominant male partner; others were more progressive and most definitely didn't. The nuances eluded me. I didn't want to hurt anybody. Perhaps that's why the lad culture of drinking and fighting enticed me. I thought that was what it meant to be a man.

I had started to listen to podcasts, some of which became increasingly influential on me, particularly Joe Rogan. Here was an older man who had achieved things in life that I thought were cool and which inspired me. Joe Rogan is a traditionally masculine bloke with a background in fighting. He goes hunting and he would invite ultra-runners on to his podcast. He would speak about the need for men to take responsibility for their lives and to make active decisions about introducing positive elements like physical activity. His messaging resonated with me. I was looking for a way out of the lifestyle I'd been living, and as I listened to Joe Rogan and others, I gradually felt that I was being offered a different perspective. It excited me. If felt as if I was receiving paternal guidance. Here was an older, successful man explaining to me how the world works. I was being shown a different path; another step on the way to a new me.

All I had to do was take it.

It happened one night when I was out with my friends in a Brighton club. I never really liked this particular club. To be honest, I never really liked clubbing at all, but I did it a lot because I felt like I had to be there. Classic. This place was sketchy, well known for drugs and house music. Not my scene. It was where my mates had chosen to go, however, and the urge to be part of a community was still strong. So there I was, drinking the evening away in an attempt to feel more comfortable in myself, to shed the notion that I didn't really want to be there. I pottered around. I awkwardly tried to dance. I wandered over to the smoking area even though I didn't smoke. The club was busy, noisy, hot. I remember looking round in a semi-drunken blur and thinking to myself: *What am I doing here? This is stupid. This is not the way I should be living.* Joe Rogan had offered me an alternative to the lad culture of drinking and gambling in which I'd become so engrossed. I thought to myself: *Maybe I can do something different.*

Maybe I can do it now.

It was two in the morning. Peak time. The club was rammed and pumping. I was dressed in jeans, a polo shirt and a pair of Nike Cortez trainers, the shoes famously worn by Forrest Gump. I didn't say goodbye to my friends. I simply walked out of the club into the mild autumn night.

And then I started to run home. Brighton to Worthing. Eleven miles.

I was 20 years old. I hadn't exercised for a long time. At first, as I ran along the Brighton seafront towards Worthing, I felt a sense of exhilaration. The pain soon kicked in. I stopped to catch my breath. Then I started running again. I took my shirt off to cool down. Then I started running again. I even stopped to sleep on the pavement for half an hour. But I still started running again. It was uncomfortable and amateurish. The seafront path between Brighton and Worthing was mercifully unpopulated at that time of night, but if anyone had seen me I would have cut an unimpressive figure as I plodded those 11 miles in the small hours of the morning. I had a stitch. I was sweating and out of breath. This was not the performance of an elite athlete at the peak of physical fitness. Compared to what I was used to, though, I felt like Usain Bolt. I kept going and somehow, after three or four hours, I was home.

In my head, I'd been searching for a means of escape from the situation in which I found myself. When I look back on that crazy run from the nightclub, I realise I was manifesting that need to escape in the simplest way I knew how. I wasn't just running away from the club. I was leaving a previous version of myself behind. I was taking yet another small step towards a different me. Literally.

. . .

My friends would not have thought that running home from the club in Brighton was particularly out of character. It fitted the narrative they had about me, and which I played up to a little: kind of weird, kind of crazy. It was just Russ being slightly unhinged, slightly reckless. A funny drunk story to tell in the pub, not so different from the time I got into a fight with the bouncers, or arrested for invading the pitch at Portsmouth. I revelled in that image. I laughed alongside them. I couldn't tell them that my oddball decision that night was the outward expression of something going on inside me. Maybe I didn't even know it myself, at the time.

Pretty soon, however, I started going for runs. Nothing heavy. I lacked the confidence to change my lifestyle completely. I just quietly and occasionally hit the pavements. Then I received a text message from my friend Jordan. He'd stopped drinking and partying. Clearly the lad culture was losing its lustre for him too. He told me that he'd signed up to run the Brighton half marathon. Was I interested in running it, so we could train alongside each other?

I played it cool. Yeah. Whatever. Inwardly, a switch flicked. Running a half marathon sounded awesome. It felt like something I could be a part of. It felt like somewhere I could belong. I no longer wanted to be drunk in clubs or lairy with strangers.

I started training. Not a lot, and I certainly relied on Jordan to keep me motivated and show me what to do. Two or three times a week we'd hit the pavements of Worthing. I was cautious about telling my other mates what I was doing, at least at first. The hardest part of stepping away from the group, and the groupthink, is taking the first step. Every step you take after that is easier. The more I ran, the more comfortable I became with the idea of missing an evening down the pub, or going out and not drinking. I began to wonder if I'd found the activity that would let me express who I was in a way that was not harmful or toxic. I liked running. I was happy doing it. I was learning that when you find something that you're passionate about, the opinions of others matter less to you. And the more steps you take, the less you care.

I ran my first half marathon in 2018 with a time of 1 hour 38 minutes. Not bad for a rookie, although Jordan beat me by a full ten minutes. The completion of that run marked a turning point for me. I was in. Completely invested. I became obsessed with training; I ran all the time and went to the gym. The full Brighton marathon was to take place six weeks later. Jordan and I signed up. I had no detailed training plan to build up to the 26-mile/ 42-kilometre run. I didn't try to overcomplicate anything. I kept it simple. I just ran until I was tired, up and down the seafront in Worthing, and little by little I improved.

My first marathon was so hard. Comfortably the hardest thing I'd ever done. I started to feel the strain at the 25-kilometre mark. By 32, I was toasted. My legs cramped. My jaw ached from gritting my teeth. But I was determined not to stop. My dad had run a couple of marathons when I was young. I remembered him saying, 'Whatever you do, don't walk. Walking is the enemy. Just keep running.' In my head, stopping to walk would have been as bad as failing to complete the run. So I didn't stop. I kept going. I finished my first marathon in 3 hours and 42 minutes. Again, not bad for a first-timer. The time, though, wasn't important. What was important was the lesson that I learned that day: the best outcomes lie on the other side of the struggle.

The experience of running that marathon was gruelling; it took everything out of me. Yet the exhilaration I felt when it was complete was unforgettable. It changed my perspective. I realised that in the years that preceded my first marathon, I'd been taking the easy path, dealing with the drudgery, disappointment and confusion of my day-to-day life in ways that required no great effort on my part. I was slowly learning, however, that the easy path now leads to the harder path later, and the hard path now leads to the easy path later. I'd taken the easy path as much as I could, trying to hide from the realities of my life by drinking too much and losing myself in the world of online gambling. By blaming other people for my problems. By kicking my issues down the road, where they would come at me when I was even more ill-equipped to meet them.

Gradually, I was learning an important fact about life: you don't get to avoid the struggle, but you do get to choose it.

For me, running was the choice.

4

HARDEST GEEZER

That's not to say I made an overnight transformation.

The summer after I ran the Brighton marathon, some friends and I took a trip to a festival in Spain. We were, it's fair to say, a little raucous. One evening at the campsite we played a drinking game called Edward Winehands. The idea of this game is that the contestants have to gaffer-tape a bottle of wine to each hand, meaning that they can't use their hands until they've drunk both bottles. I thought I was the big dog, so I swapped the bottles of wine for bottles of vodka. Carnage. We became even rowdier and the Spanish bouncers decided, quite rightly, that they'd had enough of us. One particular bouncer approached and started having a go at us. With two bottles of vodka inside me, I grabbed the gaffer tape and, before he knew what was happening, started running circles of tape all around him so he was all tightly gaffered up. He wasn't happy and his mates weren't happy. They started chasing me all through the camp. There were plenty of Brits at the festival, so lots of them helped me hide from the irate security guys, and as a result of our drunken shenanigans, our group became known as the hardest geezers.

Back home, we adopted the nickname, but we soon decided that we couldn't all be the hardest geezers. One of us had to claim that title. Two candidates emerged: me and my mate Harry. It was decided that we should contest the title by means of a boxing match. We went to the park and set up a boxing ring with some rope. We fought with gloves, but bare-chested. Neither of us were good boxers. Neither of us floated like a butterfly or stung like a bee. We just went at each other a bit clumsily, both of us desperate to win the title. I took my fair share of punches, but then I managed to knock Harry down to the ground. He staggered up to his feet and I managed to put him down again. Harry couldn't continue, and so the prize was mine. Among our little group of hardest geezers, my mates pronounced me *the* Hardest Geezer. The nickname stuck (and Harry and I remained good mates).

So, although I'd discovered a newfound interest in running, I was still one of the lads. Life wasn't quite the same as it had been before the marathon, though. I reconciled with my parents a little. They let me move back home. I quit my sales job and went back to doing cleaning, like I had before I left college. It didn't feel like a step back, though. The opposite. Having run the marathon, I started doing much better in life. My lifestyle was healthier, I wasn't going out so much, I'd stopped gambling, I hated my job less and I even started to save a bit of money. After a few months I had six grand in my bank account. I also had an idea. Things might have been improving for me, but I was still kind of sick of pottering around Worthing doing the same old stuff every day. I wanted more. I wanted to see the world, and the empowering moment arrived when I realised that there was nothing to stop me doing it.

I was so naïve. I had no understanding of how the world worked. Maybe if I had, I'd have been more daunted at the prospect of taking off by myself and wandering halfway across the globe. I bought a one-way ticket to Italy for eight quid. From there I took a flight to Egypt, my first-ever trip to the continent of Africa.

I arrived in Cairo in the middle of the night. As I stepped out for the first time into the fragrant warmth of the African night, a crowd of taxi drivers started to hassle and jostle me. I felt nervous, overwhelmed by this new and unfamiliar environment. But I felt intrigued and entranced too. I knew nothing about Egypt, its people or its culture. The craziness of the markets, where hawkers shouted and money changed hands, was new to me. The food was also unfamiliar. But I learned to hide inside when sandstorms blew through the city. I took a motorbike along narrow side streets. I saw the Pyramids of Giza. I stayed in a cheap hotel with blood-stained sheets where I made friends with the owner and sat outside with him, drinking tea and talking.

And every day I would go out running, training in this exciting new environment. In some ways, running in Africa was no different to running in Worthing. It was just a matter of putting one foot in front of another. In other ways, it was completely different. The sights, the sounds, the smells, the people. It all felt like a massive adventure, and adventure, as I was beginning to learn, was what I craved the most.

From Egypt, I hopped on a flight to Kenya. I'd heard that there was a little village where all the best Kenyan runners went to train. Its name was Iten, and it is home to a high-altitude running school that has produced an insane number of the world's greatest long-distance athletes. I wanted to visit to see how these people trained, so I took a ten-hour bus ride from Nairobi to this village. I climbed out of the bus only to realise I was the only white guy in the vicinity. I attracted some strange looks, not for the last time. I found myself a tiny hotel room that cost £6 a night and offered little in the way of comfort. When I tried to turn on the shower, it didn't work. I went to reception to explain the situation. 'No problem!' the woman told me, and she handed me a bucket of water. This was Africa, and I loved it.

It took me a week of searching around Iten to find the training school. It turned out to be a little compound full of athletes. Many Kenyans, of course, but also a fair few Europeans, including Team GB athletes. I stayed there for several weeks, training with this collection of unreal runners, all way better than me. They lived simple, almost monastic lives, which I emulated. I had a tiny room with a single bed and no furnishings or other comforts. I hand-washed my clothes in a bucket and hung them out on a bush to dry. I ate simple African food in a communal eating space twice a day – high-carb staples of bread, rice and pap (a kind of thick porridge), with only the occasional bit of meat. I learned what it meant to focus 100 per cent on training without the usual distractions of modern living. That mindset appealed to me. I liked the way that they were totally focused on their goal of becoming the best runners they could be. It had a purity. In the UK, the excesses of Western culture had almost been my downfall. Here on the east coast of Africa, I was being shown another way. Many of these African runners saw their sport as a way out. They were using running to change their lives, just as I was. I'd join them on runs at five in the morning, before the heat of the day kicked in, and find myself unable to keep up with the pack for more than a few minutes. A humbling experience, but I consoled myself that I'd only really been running seriously for a year, whereas these people had devoted their lives to the sport. From that perspective, perhaps I wasn't doing too badly.

I decided I wanted to see some more of Kenya. I visited Mombasa, then Diani, where I stayed in a hostel on the beach. It was here that I met a man who planted a seed in my mind. His name was Giovanni. He was an Italian who had been cycling around the world for the previous six years. All he had with him was his bike and a rucksack with a few essentials: a tent, a sleeping bag, a few clothes, a phone he barely used and, most important of all, a little pot for brewing coffee. I thought he was the coolest guy I'd ever met. He had stripped his life back to the fundamentals and he was challenging himself not because he was wanted fame or fortune, but for the purity of the challenge itself.

Any Westerner who has ever been to the continent of Africa will know that it is not like anywhere else. You experience a culture shock. For some people, the change of environment has longer-lasting effects. I think I was one of those people. The form-filling, bureaucratic nature of life in the UK held little attraction for me. Here in Kenya, especially away from the more built-up areas, life was stripped down to the bare necessities. In the UK, if a person wants to build a house, they enter a nightmare of permissions and regulations and paperwork. In Africa, they find four sheets of something that stands up straight and put a roof on it. In the UK, to get from A to B requires expense and multiple modes of transport. In Africa, they chuck ten people in an old car and they're good to go. Admittedly, a lot of this has to do with poverty, but the first-principles approach to life in the remoter regions appealed to me. There was a sense that anything was possible.

Africa changed me in other ways too. Perhaps I didn't realise it at the time, but looking back now I understand that my time in Kenya especially crystallised in my mind certain elements of life to which I was attracted: simplicity, high performance and challenge. After spending time in the training camp and talking to Giovanni, I found myself examining the map of the world on my phone and wondering if I too could construct a challenge worth undertaking. I'd proved to myself that there was nothing stopping me from leaving the UK and travelling wherever I wanted. I'd exposed myself to the idea that anything is possible, if you strip away all the extraneous stuff and simply put your mind to it. I knew I loved endurance and running. My gaze fell on Istanbul and I wondered if it would be possible to run from there all the way across Europe and back to London. Marathons every day. Carrying nothing but what I needed. Challenging myself daily.

The idea stuck. It wouldn't go away.

I continued my travels. My plan was to go from Kenya to India. I rolled up at the airport in Nairobi and was asked for my visa and yellow fever certificate. My what? I didn't know anything about yellow fever or visas. The person at the counter told me to go and see an airport doctor. I handed the doctor £25 and in return the doctor gave me a yellow fever certificate and escorted me to the plane. When we stopped over in Dubai, they checked my documents again. My hooky yellow fever certificate had the wrong dates written on it, and of course there was still no visa for India. It was not the last time my plans would be scuppered by visa problems. I wasn't allowed on the next plane, but I was free to stay in Dubai, so that's what I did. From Dubai I went to Thailand and from there to Australia. I knew I was going to run out of money soon, and I could get work in Australia to replenish my funds. I took a job picking and packing in a factory, then signed myself up for a medical trial where they gave me my board and lodging for a couple of weeks while they tested a new drug on me and paid me £4,000. I was buzzing, because I knew that money would pay for the idea that I had been gestating in my mind. The idea of running from Istanbul to London.

• • •

Keep it simple. That was my mantra. I suppose I could have researched in pernickety detail the best route to take if I wanted to run from Asia to London. I suppose I could have spoken to ultra-runners who'd done something similar, and planned everything in minute detail.

I did none of that.

While I was still in Australia I opened up Google Maps, typed in Istanbul to London and tapped on the little icon that indicated a walking route. Within a few seconds, the familiar blue line appeared, starting in Turkey and cutting through Europe. I could have assembled a team and planned places to stay along the way but I didn't have the funds or the temperament for that. I simply turned the prospect over in my head and tried to work out what I would need. I'd rock up in Istanbul, run a marathon and then I'd need somewhere to sleep. A hammock would be lighter than a tent, so I decided to pack one of those. I'd probably need two sets of clothes, so I could sleep in one outfit and run in it the next day, then change into my second set of clothes and wash the first. I'd need a phone and a power bank to charge it. I'd need a head torch, earphones and a rain mac. A bar of soap, a toothbrush and some toothpaste. That was it. Anything else would be an unnecessary luxury. I certainly wouldn't need a razor blade. I'd always wanted a beard but hadn't been able to grow one until I was in my twenties. I started out with a little chin strap, but when I went travelling I let it grow more freely. By now I had a big orange beard, and I planned to keep it.

I was staying with my friends Kyle and Summer in Australia as I made these calculations. I told them my plan. They estimated my chance of death at 30 per cent. I laughed. Sure, I had never run a back-to-back marathon, let alone the 70 or so I figured it would take me to become the first person to run from Asia to London. But what was the worst that could happen? Kyle and Summer weren't the only people to think I was nuts. Everyone else I mentioned it to thought that the idea was unhinged. I shrugged off their concerns. My head was in a different place to them. I thought it was totally do-able. I'd done weeks when I'd run 200 kilometres, which averaged out at about 30 kilometres a day – not so far from the 42 kilometres a marathon required. It would be painful, but I was close enough.

More importantly, I'd decided to approach my life in a whole different way.

Before, back in England, I'd felt trapped by my situation. I kept trying to take the next little step outside of it, but never had the vision to think bigger than that. From now on, I would shoot for the best possible outcome, then work out what might stop me from achieving it and try to overcome those little niggles as they arose. Now I could imagine something, and it might seem completely mad, but if I believed it was possible I knew I could find a way to deal with the obstacles.

So people might have thought I was stupid, but I thought *they* were stupid. They were thinking too small. They couldn't see the bigger picture.

I decided to go for it.

5

CONTINENTAL GEEZER

ignored the naysayers and flew to Istanbul with only the few possessions I would need to make my first attempt at ultra-running. Istanbul is a city geographically divided in two by the Bosporus Strait. The Bosporus is 700 metres wide at its narrowest point and traditionally marks a dividing line between Asia and Europe. If I wanted my run to start in Asia, it meant I needed start on the eastern side of the Bosporus. A suspension bridge, busy with traffic, spans the waterway. The bridge has no pavement and it's illegal for pedestrians to cross, which left me with one option: to swim.

I mean, throw me in a pool and tell me to stay alive and I'll probably make it to the side with a lot of splashing and an embarrassing amount of doggy paddle, but I'm no Michael Phelps. I'd grown fond of challenging myself, though, so I packaged up my gear into a bin bag, tied it to my ankle and, wearing nothing but a pair of shorts, jumped into the Bosporus.

Swimming a major waterway with a bin bag tied to your ankle is hard enough even for a competent swimmer. I hadn't, however, quite anticipated the strength of the current. It was incredibly powerful. I'd have struggled even in still waters. The current whipped me all over the place. The Bosporus is a bustling body of water, one of the busiest shipping lanes in the world, and at one point I nearly got hit by a fast-moving ferry. Not good. In fact, it made me begin to think that this wasn't my best idea. A real don't-try-this-at-home-kids moment.

Did I mention that it's also illegal to swim in the Bosporus? Well, it is. Maybe that's why nobody else was doing it. By the time I was two thirds of the way across – spluttering, struggling and doggy-paddling – the local police force had been alerted to my presence. A speedboat full of armed police sped up to me, and before I knew it I was staring the wrong way down the barrels of several big guns. The police barked at me to get into the boat and I didn't have much choice but to do what they said. I clambered over the side and hauled in the bag tied to my ankle. The police were pretty pissed off with me, but they did escort me to the western side of the Bosporus, where they ejected me from the speedboat with strong arms and ferocious glares. Then they sped off again and left me, soaking and a bit shaken up, to start running.

So that's what I did. I ran.

Google Maps was my guide. I ran a cheeky marathon, following the map to a suburb where I camped for my first night. I knew that night-times were potentially dangerous, so I tried to be smart about where I stopped. I preferred to be away from the public gaze, but not too far from a town or village in case I needed the security of a more built-up area. My hammock, though, meant that I required trees, which limited my choices. As I slung my hammock between two trees in the suburbs of Istanbul that night,

I heard the call to prayer from a nearby mosque. It wasn't the first time I'd heard that evocative sound – the call to prayer had been sounded in Cairo during my visit but I hadn't known what it was then, and I didn't know what it was now. Why were they singing tunes across the town? My ignorance showed how little I knew about the world. It showed how much I had to learn. As I lay in my hammock, locals drove up and shone their lights at me. I was a curiosity and they wanted to take a look. Thankfully they let me be, and I eventually fell asleep.

I awoke the next morning with the usual aches and pains to be expected the day after running a marathon. Now I had to run another. I'd never run back-to-back marathons before. Today would be the first time. I was full of adrenaline. Full of determination. As I tied up my shoelaces that morning, I remembered the years I'd spent after leaving home, worrying that it might be true that I'd never do anything with my life. I'd walked away from my parents' house at the age of 17 thinking that I was going to smash it. A regular Charlie Big Potatoes. Life was going to be great, I told myself. It hadn't turned out that way. I'd endured a pretty tough few years. I thought I'd kill it in sales; I hated it and went back to cleaning. I thought I'd make a big success of my relationship, marry and settle down; it didn't work out. I'd lost myself to gambling and had to move back into my parents' house, skint. I knew what people were thinking: that my life was following a predictably disastrous path. In my head, this run was my chance to prove everybody wrong.

Plenty of people still doubted me. I'd posted to my handful of followers on social media that I was running home from Istanbul.

Someone commented that they guaranteed I wouldn't get past day 40. Such comments lit the fire inside me. Some of the rage I'd experienced as a younger man returned, but now I had a way of harnessing it for a positive purpose. I had a point to prove. I'd already fucked things up once. There was no way I would fuck things up again. No way I would quit. I was willing to put myself through anything to get it done. I didn't care about the aches and pains. I didn't care about the naysayers. I only cared about the mission I'd set myself.

I only cared about redemption.

I completed the marathon on my second day. I proved to myself that it could be done. After that, it was just a question of rinsing and repeating.

My route through Europe from Istanbul crossed 11 countries: Turkey, Bulgaria, Serbia, Hungary, Austria, Czech Republic, Germany, Netherlands, Belgium, France and the UK. The terrain was mostly flat, as I kept to the north of the Alps, although I did have to cross the Balkan mountains in Bulgaria. I could only carry a litre and a half of water at a time, so it was necessary to replenish my supply from taps or streams along the way. My main source of fuel was nuts, because they were light and dense in calories, and ice creams from petrol stations where I would stop of an evening to charge my phone before finding somewhere to camp. The nuts and ice cream formed 70 per cent of my diet. I had no money to eat in restaurants, so the remaining 30 per cent came from baked goods in supermarkets along the way. I barely ate any hot food. There was no bespoke nutritional plan. I just had to get the calories in.

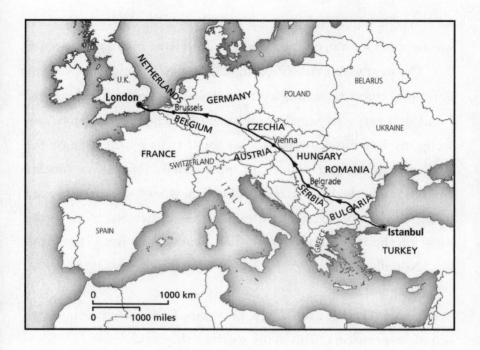

My body felt the strain as the days passed and the marathons accumulated. My knees, ankles and hips hurt. I experienced extreme muscle fatigue in my legs, quads, calves and Achilles tendons. My only strategy was to push on through it. Blisters appeared on my feet. They stung, but I figured that if I was to worry about blisters, I was in the wrong game. In any case, I discovered that the discomfort tended to ease off into a slight tingle after half an hour of running.

At first, I had nothing to keep me warm at night. A heatwave pounded Europe that summer, but sometimes it grew bitterly cold after sundown, so I added an extra item to my scant inventory: a jumper. When it became clear that even with a jumper I was freezing cold at night, I swapped it for a sleeping bag. It made for more comfortable nights, but it was a pain during the day because there was no room for it in my backpack, so I had to tie it around my waist.

The heatwave made life tough. One day in Bulgaria I ran my daily marathon in 40-degree heat. I was completely exhausted. I had no energy to hunt around for a better place to sleep, so I slung my hammock between two small trees by the side of the road. Before long, a police car approached. Two police officers emerged and asked me, in broken English, what I was doing. I tried to explain in non-existent Bulgarian that I intended to sleep the night by the road. They shook their heads. 'Not here,' they told me. 'Not allowed.'

'Why not?'

They looked at each other. Then they looked back at me with serious expressions. 'Too many wolves,' they said.

They watched me while I packed up my hammock and started walking down the road. Then they climbed back in the car and drove away. I wasn't exactly keen to be hunted by wolves, but I was so knackered from running in the heatwave that there was no way I could walk very far. After a kilometre or so, I came across an apple tree farm. I sneaked in and slung my hammock between two apple trees, lay down and tried to rest my drained body and get some shuteye. Fat chance. As the sun set and the moon rose, I heard howls in the vicinity. The policemen were right. I could tell that the wolves were close, but I was committed to my sleeping place now. There was no way I could risk breaking camp and walking through the forest to find a safer place. So I lay there all night, shivering and barely dozing. Every half hour a howl would echo through the trees, and in my half-awake state it felt like they were circling, running all around me, closing in. I also couldn't shake my anxiety that I was trespassing on somebody's farm and would wake up with a shotgun in my mouth. I was relieved when morning came and I could strike camp and put some miles between me and the unseen threats.

One night in Hungary, when I'd finished my marathon for the day and was looking for somewhere to sling my hammock, I saw a signpost for a campsite a kilometre in the distance. A campsite always felt like a safer option than slinging my hammock in the wild, so I headed in that direction. A woman approached me as I was walking and started chatting in Hungarian with only a few words of English. It wasn't too unusual to have locals coming up to talk to me. I probably looked a bit unusual to them, and they wanted to know what I was doing. This woman, though, was more persistent than most. She wasn't in the least put off by my inability to speak Hungarian. I was pretty certain that she wasn't trying to chat me up in the ordinary way. After all, I was in a bit of a state: I was knackered after the day's run and, having been on the road for a good 30 days without washing properly, I surely presented a rather disgusting figure. Not much of a catch. So I guessed that she was a local prostitute, touting for business and unwilling to take no for an answer.

I reached the campsite with the woman still at my side, still talking, still refusing to leave me alone. The campsite owner refused me entry. He said they were full but I knew that wasn't true because I could see loads of empty pitches. Plenty of room for an exhausted runner and his hammock. It seemed obvious to me that they recognised the prostitute and thought I was trying to bring her into the campsite. I tried to explain that I didn't know her, that she was nothing to do with me, but my language skills weren't up to the task and they didn't care anyway. They were adamant. They turned me away.

It was dark now. The woman was still with me, still following me, still talking. She found a few hesitant words of heavily accented English. 'I give you … blowjob?'

I shook my head. 'Nah,' I said, and I kept on walking.

'I give you blowjob!'

I pulled out my phone. Found a picture of me and a female friend back home. 'My girlfriend,' I said. 'Me and my girlfriend …'

Either she didn't understand what I was saying, or she didn't care. She grabbed my arm and tried to drag me into some bushes at the side of the road. 'Me and you, in the bush! Blowjob!'

I shook my head again. Kept on walking. She tried to lead me down various deserted paths, but I resisted. I could tell she was getting annoyed. She started shouting at me. 'You waste my time,' she yelled. 'You owe me money!'

'You've wasted your own time,' I told her. It didn't go down well. She took out her phone and made a call. Yapped away to someone in Hungarian. I couldn't understand what she was saying, of course, but I could interpret her tone of voice. I knew it wasn't a good phone call from my perspective. I reckoned she was complaining to her pimp. This was clearly not an ideal situation. I didn't want an aggressive Hungarian pimp to pull up in a car and start demanding money. So I did the only thing I could think of: I legged it.

The prostitute chased me, but I suppose I had a bit of an advantage. I remembered seeing a motorway maybe a kilometre in the distance, so I headed for that, leaving her far behind. I jumped over the barriers, crossed the motorway and found a couple of trees to sling my hammock by the side of the road. My phone had died. I was worried that the prostitute's pimp would be circling around trying to find me. Frankly, I'd have preferred the wolves. I didn't sleep well that night either.

I woke the next morning with a dead phone and no real idea where I was. I wandered for a bit and found a public bathroom where the mirrors were cracked and shattered. I remember looking at my distorted reflection and thinking that this was a real low point. I washed in the sink, then managed to find my way back to the route I'd been following the night before. I ran all day and ended up at a petrol station where a lovely Hungarian bloke gave me a cold beer and a hot shower. He let me charge my phone. I opened up Google Maps and realised I was halfway home. From a low moment to a high in the space of 12 hours. The pendulum could swing fast, I was learning, during a mission like this.

In Serbia, I was fast asleep in the middle of the night when I suddenly thudded to the ground. Not good. I heard the scurrying of footsteps and smelled the scent of something burning. Adrenaline flooded through me as I scrambled to my knees and peered into the darkness to see silhouettes disappearing. It turned out that a bunch of teenagers had thought it would be a laugh to burn the ropes that tied my hammock to the tree and let me fall. Cheers, lads.

The wolves, the prostitutes, the arson-inclined teenagers ... at times I was scared, but mostly I thrived on the excitement and adventure of it all. For the main part, and especially in Eastern Europe, I benefitted from the kindness of strangers. I rolled up at a village inn in Turkey at ten o'clock one evening, completely done over by the day's run. A man in the pub invited me into his family home and gave me a bed for the night. In Serbia, I knocked on a stranger's door to ask if I could charge my phone. I ended up camping in the garden and the lady of the house brought me a welcome plate of hot dinner. The further west I ran, and the closer I got to home, I found people a little less friendly, a little less interested in what I was doing. I just kept on going, marathon after marathon. When the time came to cross the English Channel, I arranged for a treadmill on the ferry to make up the miles of the crossing. I landed in Dover and ran straight to London via Gravesend. I arrived there after 66 days, several days quicker than I'd expected. Somehow, though, it didn't feel quite right finishing my mission in the capital. I'd set out on my travels several months earlier from Worthing, so I decided to spend a couple more days running from London to the south coast.

I didn't have many followers on social media when I started out. Maybe 150 people on Instagram, mostly my friends from Worthing. I thought it would be cool to document what I was doing as I ran across Europe. My posts started getting shared around a bit, and by the time I'd finished I had perhaps 5,000 followers.

This had two consequences. The first was that I had the opportunity to raise a bit of money for a cause that was important to me. The Running Charity exists to use running as a means to empower young people who are struggling with a variety of issues. They believe that health and fitness can be the spark that changes a lot of young people's lives. It resonated with me, because I felt it aligned with the journey I'd been on and I knew that, along with the right guidance, running could help a lot of other people. As a result of my small following, I managed to raise a few thousand pounds for the charity.

It also meant that somewhere between 50 and 100 people joined me for the final five kilometres. It was surreal, having set out on my own 68 days ago in Istanbul to the withering glances of a few angry Turkish policemen, to have a crowd at my back as I returned to my hometown. And it felt surreal to be back. I'd left Worthing a year ago hoping to see a bit of the world, with no idea that the trip would end this way. The weeks I'd spent running felt like a lifetime. It was a peculiar homecoming.

Mission completed, I went straight to the pub for one of the best pints of my life. That evening, my friends and I went to a local club for a bit of a party.

And that night I ran back home.

6

PRISON GEEZER

In some ways, I felt that my life had completely changed after the run from Asia to London. I'd proved to myself and to others that I was capable of achieving what I set out to do. I'd ticked off a few boxes on my internal scorecard. I'd accomplished something of note. In other ways, however, I felt I'd come full circle. I hadn't totally paid off my gambling debts, and I'd funded the mission off credit cards. So now I was skint, jobless and homeless and back in Worthing. I asked my parents if I could stay at their house for a bit. They agreed. The old tensions remained, however, so I soon moved into a flat with a friend. My plan was to save up enough money to kickstart another mission. Asia to London had given me a taste for ultra running. Now I wanted to step it up a notch. I wanted to run across Australia. I worked a few bar jobs and as a delivery driver. I even lined up a couple of clinical trials to give me a nice little top-up and earn my passage Down Under. Everything was going nicely to plan.

And then Covid hit.

Those days were so tough for so many people in so many ways. I found them difficult because at that time I had just newly understood the possibilities of the world. I did not need to be boxed in by my own limitations, or the limitations of others. The world was out there to be conquered. There were places to see and adventures to be had. I could go anywhere and do anything.

Except now I couldn't.

The prospect of sitting at home watching Netflix held no attraction for me. I decided that, if I had to be in the UK, I would use the time to do something interesting. I wanted a new experience, something that would take me out of my self-isolation and into a different environment. So I decided to take a job as a prison officer.

My shifts would start at 7.30am, which meant turning up at 7.15 to allow enough time to pass through security. We officers weren't allowed to take anything into the prison with us, so I'd stow my stuff in a locker before heading to the gate and showing my ID. I'd pick up a radio and a set of keys then pass through an airlock – a room with two doors, which were never allowed to be open at the same time – into the main part of the prison. There were no high-tech airport scanners to check that we officers weren't smuggling anything in. As a result, the prisoners were able to acquire plenty of contraband – mostly drugs – courtesy of any officer who wanted to make a few quid on the side. It was easy money. There'd be occasional spot checks and body searches, but the prison security was lacking. On one occasion, I was offered five grand to bring a package in for one of the prisoners. I declined. The sentence for smuggling in contraband was ten years, and a decade of bird did not feature in my future plans.

Covid affected prisons as much as anywhere else. More, even. The prison was much more closed than it might otherwise have been. In ordinary times, prisoners would be allowed to go to the gym or the exercise yard. If they were well behaved, they could have jobs. The Covid regulations banned all that. Inmates found themselves banged up for 23½ hours a day, with half an hour to eat some food and take 15 minutes of fresh air. Hardly surprising that many of them struggled.

During my prison-officer training, the instructors emphasised the importance of rehabilitation and empathy in our dealings with the inmates. Fine words, but the reality of life in prison, especially during Covid, was very different. With six to eight officers on a wing of 150 prisoners, it was a struggle just to ensure that the inmates received the basics: food and a little time in the yard. Once those essentials were covered, and a few people had inevitably kicked off, there was hardly time to sit down and have morale-boosting chats. To be a prison officer was to fight fires daily.

I was by no means the hardest geezer in that place. The first time I stepped onto the wing, I felt pretty intimidated. As time passed, however, I found it quite easy to relate to a lot of the prisoners. Many of them weren't so different to me and my own mates, and part of me understood that if I'd continued on the path I'd started to tread before running diverted me, I might have ended up in their situation.

In my first week, I walked into a cell to find an inmate having a seizure on the floor. The drug spice is endemic in prison. People call it synthetic weed, but it is more like synthetic heroin. This was a spice-induced seizure and I thought he was going to die. Soon after that, I encountered a guy who'd sliced his neck with a razor and was bleeding out on the landing.

The smallest disagreements could evolve into dangerous scenarios. One morning three fellow officers and I filed into a meeting with our manager to be told that a situation was brewing over an Xbox. These were a privilege for good behaviour, but on this occasion a notoriously hard inmate had stolen one of the other guy's consoles and was refusing to return it. Our job was to enter his cell to retrieve the Xbox and then return it. The inmate in question was an absolute unit: six foot five, 18 stone and fond of a scrap. We looked at each other and almost giggled at the chances of this going smoothly.

We crossed the landing and stood outside the prisoner's cell. My colleague knocked on the door and opened it up. The prisoner lay on his bed, arms behind his head.

'Did you take the Xbox?' my colleague asked him.

'Yeah.'

'You're going to have to give it back.'

The unit shook his head. 'No,' he growled.

We entered. My colleague saw the Xbox and grabbed it. The unit jumped out of his bed, ripped the Xbox from my colleague's hands and smacked him over the head with it.

We had no choice. We piled in and manhandled this guy to the floor. More officers arrived. The bloke was so big, and he struggled so fiercely, that it took all six or seven of us to restrain him. I remember grabbing his tree trunk of a leg, holding on and hoping for the best. Eventually we managed to wrap him up and march him down to the segregation unit. Not an easy job.

He was not even the scariest guy I had to deal with. At least his hostility was predictable. It was the unpredictable inmates who presented a tougher problem. One guy could be the friendliest man in the world one day, and the next day he would try to rip your head off. He'd be completely fine when we told him it was time to leave the exercise yard and return to his cell, but when he reached the cell door he'd refuse to enter. We'd try to talk him round. It never worked and he invariably lashed out at us. We'd end up having to get physical with him. In my first week alone I ended up in four or five bust-ups with men like him. I learned that some situations required submissiveness and de-escalation. Others required dominance. I developed an instinct for these different scenarios, little knowing that the time would come – in the not-too-distant future but many thousands of miles away – that this instinct might well save my life.

Prison life makes a person appreciate their freedoms. At least, it made this person appreciate his. Being a prison officer is a hard job, but it's not as hard as being a prisoner. One morning, I was unlocking the cells so the prisoners could take some exercise. I opened up one cell to see the inmate had torn up some sheets, knotted them together and tried to hang himself. Somehow I didn't feel shocked or upset. I just focused on finding a solution. I jumped into the cell, grabbed the prisoner by his legs and held him to loosen the strain on his makeshift noose. Another prisoner entered the cell and together we lowered him onto the ground. I thought at first that he was dead, but we'd arrived just in time. He lived. A few weeks later, the same inmate was in the segregation ward, the area that houses inmates in solitary confinement and those on suicide watch, which means they have to have a guard with them at all times. I was that guard, and I chatted to the inmate at length. He was in denial about his suicide attempt, and barely anything he said made sense to me. His problems were so deep and complex that it was hard to understand what was going on in his head. The prison walls enclosed him, but so did the broken walls of his own mind. It made me appreciate even more my own freedom to go where I wanted and follow my own pursuits.

Working in prison hardened me up. It's easy, sometimes, for us to overreact to the small inconveniences of life. For the men in that prison, life truly was difficult. And when you've rescued a prisoner who has tried to hang himself, or pinned an angry geezer to the floor, or witnessed men helpless with drug addiction, or seen an entire wing locked down because of a Covid outbreak so that the prisoners can only receive their food from guards like me in hazmat suits, it changes your perspective on life. Having tasted the freedom of travel, my stint as a prison guard gave me an insight into what life might be like if that freedom was taken away.

That insight made me all the more determined to seek adventure wherever I could.

· · ·

The run from Istanbul to London had given me a taste for challenging myself. I started casting around for other projects that I could pursue in the UK. The idea of running up mountains intrigued me, so on several occasions I ran up Ben Nevis, Scafell Pike and Snowdon. They're the three highest peaks in Scotland, England and Wales respectively, but in global terms they're kind of diddy, so I didn't put in any extra training for them. I would just rock up at the weekend or having taken a day off work, sometimes alone, sometimes with my brother, and up we'd run.

Occasionally I'd indulge in slightly less sensible challenges. Some people whiled away their Covid lockdowns perfecting sourdough, but I ran a marathon during which I drank a bottle of Corona beer after every mile. No water. Just beer. Turns out it's not the easiest way to run a marathon. I threw up at least four times thanks to all that gassy liquid bouncing around inside me. My tolerance to alcohol was still quite high thanks to my earlier years of heavy drinking, but the running dehydrated me badly. By mile number six I was already tipsy. By halfway I could hardly run straight. The remaining 13 miles are difficult to remember. The next day I had to be at work in the prison at a quarter past seven in the morning. I hadn't mentioned to anybody that I was running a beer marathon, so I hid for the whole day and made sure I didn't have to talk to a single soul. I was certainly in no state to manhandle prisoners in and out of their cells.

Some of my challenges were less laddish. I learned that the swimmer Ross Edgley had run a marathon pulling a car in about 19 hours. He was a big guy, a successful endurance athlete who had also swum around the UK. This meant he had the muscular build of a swimmer rather than a runner, and I thought to myself: *I bet I can run a marathon pulling a car faster than him.*

I figured that the hardest part of pulling a car is getting it going. Once you've overcome that initial inertia and the wheels are rolling, it shouldn't be that bad so long as you're on the flat. What

I needed, therefore, was flat terrain and as long a stretch as possible, so that I didn't have to change direction too often, and so be obliged to restart the car. The seafront at Worthing fitted the bill. I'd need to add a bit more muscle so that I could get the car started, but a feat like that would surely be more about endurance than strength. If I carried on doing my long-distance training alongside some gym work, I'd be in with a chance.

I practised with a Peugeot 206, and I strapped myself to the car using a harness. At first I tried to pull it from my shoulders, which didn't really work. Then I tried to pull it from my hips. No luck. I soon worked out that the most efficient arrangement was to strap myself to the car from my shoulders *and* my hips, so I could brace myself, lean forward a little and engage my entire torso. I located a stretch of quiet road in Goring where I trained whenever the Covid regulations allowed it. I was somewhat known around Worthing for the Asia to London run, so while I did attract a few funny looks in training, I wasn't a complete curiosity. I trained for a good six months while holding down my job in the prison, and by the time I was able to manage a 28-kilometre run strapped to the Peugeot 206, I reckoned I was ready to attempt the full 42 kilometres of the marathon.

Having trained with the Peugeot, I attempted the full marathon with a Suzuki that belonged to a friend of mine. That car and I had history. My friends had driven it to Belgium to see me on the Asia to London run. The year before that, during the football World Cup, we'd spray-painted it with an England flag. I didn't choose it for nostalgic reasons, though. The Suzuki was much lighter than the Peugeot I'd been training with. I had to have somebody behind the wheel all the time I was pulling the car, so I persuaded my mates to take two-hour shifts. It meant that, including the driver, I was pulling a weight of about 850 kilograms.

I initially received permission from the council to use a one-kilometre stretch of the pedestrian walkway along Worthing seafront for the attempt. With two days to go, they rescinded that permission because they said they couldn't guarantee people's safety. There was no way I intended to back out now, so I started the run at two in the morning when I knew that any busybody council officer would be snugly tucked up in bed. I hauled the Suzuki into motion and pulled it along the almost deserted seafront. When I completed my first kilometre, I turned round to stop the car rolling forward with my hands. Then I unclipped the harness and attached myself to the rear of the car, so I didn't have to go through the effort of turning it around, and pulled it backwards to the starting point. Two kilometres down. Only another 40 to go …

It was ten in the morning and I was 30 kilometres in, with a crowd of onlookers urging me on, when a council guy in a hi-viz vest trundled up to me in a little buggy. He waited until I was unclipping my harness to turn around, then he marched up to me. 'You know you're not supposed to be doing this?'

'I ain't stopping now, mate,' I told him. 'Why don't you come back a bit later when we're done?'

He glanced at the crowd supporting me. I guess he realised that he'd be snubbing out the party if he was too much of a jobsworth. Fair play to the guy: he let me get on with it.

I finished the marathon in 9 hours and 56 minutes. World record. Job done. Then I went to the pub and had a few beers with the lads.

And the next day I was back in prison.

7

COFFIN GEEZER

'd only ever intended the prison job to be a stop-gap, a way of marking time while the Covid restrictions stopped me from travelling. I thought it would be an interesting way to spend a few months, but I knew that it wasn't for me as a full-time career. Being a prison officer is a bit like being in the army – there's a hierarchy and you're expected to follow orders – and people either take to it or they don't. The churn rate is high. Following orders isn't really my thing, and after 12 months, I'd had enough.

Instead, I started a little business. I had about 5,000 followers on Instagram thanks to the Asia to London run, and I could tell there was interest in my adventures up and down the mountains of the British Isles. For my new side hustle, I invited people to join me on these adventures. My repertoire comprised two trips. The first was three peaks in three days. We'd climb my new friends Ben Nevis, Scafell Pike and Snowdon, and camp in between. Slightly more hardcore was the same three peaks in 24 hours. Gruelling for my clients, and especially gruelling for me because I did all the driving on no sleep. I took out a loan and bought myself a little van that used to be a school bus. I'd pick my clients up and we'd drive straight to Scotland, where we'd stay the night. First thing in the morning we'd climb Ben Nevis, which would take four or five hours depending on the speed of the slowest climber. Then I'd drive us south to Scafell Pike in the Lake District, which we'd climb in about three hours. Then I'd drive us to Snowdon, which we'd climb as well, before I drove all round the country dropping people back home. For me, it meant being awake for 40 hours of climbing and driving. Pretty brutal.

I think it's fair to say that I was not your traditional mountain guide. I didn't know much about the technical side of mountaineering. We didn't stop to identify obscure wildflowers or learn how to make fire from tinder and kindling. My skills lay more in creating a vibe and ensuring everyone had a good time. We'd take a few beers with us and blast some music on the way. From time to time we'd jump off a cliff into a lake and just have a bit of a laugh. We climbed in all weathers. Only occasionally did I have to turn the group back, and I didn't like doing it. On one of those occasions, we were nearing the summit of Snowdon when we encountered winds of 80 miles per hour and everyone was freezing cold. On another, a blizzard hit while we were on Ben Nevis and we found ourselves in the middle of a total whiteout. In general, though, there was a good appetite for these feats of endurance and my side hustle brought in a few quid. It also enabled me to help out The Running Charity, who I'd raised money for during the Asia to London run. I worked for them, taking young people on adventures and, hopefully, showing them that fitness could have a positive impact on their lives, just as it had on mine.

• • •

In 2021, I went to a birthday party. A young woman was there who I didn't recognise. I couldn't take my eyes off her. Her name was Emily. I turned to my friend. 'How come I've never seen her before?' I asked. It turned out that she was from Shoreham, not Worthing, and we only had one mutual friend. We chatted a little bit, and I was smitten.

I tried for months after that party to persuade Emily to come on a date with me, but I don't think she really considered me a serious person, the kind of person she would date. She had a little boy, which meant real responsibilities. I lived with my mate in a flat. I didn't have a proper, secure job. I wasn't earning loads of money. I suppose I could see her point of view. While she was looking after her son, I was pulling cars along the seafront, or staggering drunk round a running track. I was also becoming intrigued by other types of endurance that I guess marked me out as being an unsuitable partner.

I enjoyed watching the illusionist David Blaine and was particularly taken with his stunt of being buried alive with no food for seven days in an underground plastic box in New York. I thought that was pretty sick. I also thought it sounded extremely hard. My run from Istanbul to London had shown me that I was able to manage a certain type of endurance, but this was something completely different and I wanted to know what it was all about. I decided I'd try to do something similar. Not in New York, of course, but in Worthing. I mean, if David Blaine could do it, surely the Hardest Geezer could do it too.

I wasn't too worried about the fasting aspect of the challenge. I'd been intermittent fasting for a few months. Partly it was because

I felt my body benefitted from that regime. Partly it was because I relished the challenge of a three- or four-day fast. The bigger problem I had was that to replicate David Blaine's stunt exactly would cost hundreds of thousands of pounds. I only had a few quid, so I had to come up with a way of cutting costs. The first challenge was finding somewhere to do it. Living in a flat, I didn't have a garden, so that was a no-go. I considered trying to do it in a public space, but my experience with the council trying to ban my car marathon told me that I'd doubtless encounter a certain amount of resistance. Even if they did grant permission, it would take for ever and I was impatient just to get on with it. All this meant I had to find a private bit of land, so I asked around my friends who had gardens. 'Will you let me bury myself alive in your lawn?'

The response was always the same. 'What if you die? We'll be liable. So: no!'

I could see their point. Eventually, though, I put up an appeal on Instagram, offering to pay a couple of hundred quid to anybody who'd let me bury myself in their lawn, and a lady in Partridge Green, not far from Worthing, took me up on the offer.

I dug a massive hole in her garden, two or three metres deep and the same in length and width. It took me at least a week with a shovel – a feat of endurance all of its own. By the time I'd finished, once I stood in the bottom it was really quite difficult to clamber out. Perfect. My next job was to find something in which to entomb myself. I ordered a rather tinny metal storage box: the length of a coffin, about a metre wide and just about big enough for me to sit up in. My mates and I placed the box into the hole and we ran a tube into it for oxygen. I planned not to eat for seven days, but I would need to drink, so we loaded it with plastic bottles of water. Then I climbed into the box. My mates replaced the lid and then backfilled the hole with the dislodged soil. I lay there, listening to the sound of dirt being shovelled onto the tin roof. The sound became more muffled as the soil level rose. My friends' voices receded. I was alone, three metres below the ground.

I was livestreaming the stunt, so I had a little light with me. But it's hot underground, and I was soon sweating heavily. Fortunately I'd stashed enough water to keep me hydrated, and I could use the empty bottles to piss into. Since I was fasting, I didn't need to shit.

I failed, however, to account for the possibility of rain.

The ground in which I'd buried myself was clay. As the rain fell, it soaked up moisture. The soil became heavier and heavier. It started to press in on the tin box. The wall and the roof started to creak and buckle. It became apparent that my metal coffin was in no way strong enough to withstand the pressure. Every now and then, some mud would leak through the sides of the box. I wasn't too worried. I knew that I had mates at ground level and that they'd soon dig me out if I gave them the word. After about 30 hours, the bottom of the coffin started filling up with water. I had electrical equipment with me for the livestream and I had to come to terms with the fact that I wasn't going to be able to stay down there for another six days if the water continued to leak in. So I pulled the plug. My friends dug me out and I emerged into the daylight.

I hated giving up. It sat badly with me. I was beginning to learn, however, that there was a financial cost associated with these missions I'd started to set myself. Having paid the lady for the use of her garden, and having paid for the metal box and all the associated costs, I was now skint. It took me another three or four months to replenish my funds for a second attempt. Three months to also work out how I was going to stop the water leaking in. The obvious answer was to get a strong, watertight box professionally made. Not possible. I just didn't have the cash. I needed another plan. If the rain was the problem, I needed to bury myself somewhere the rain couldn't get to me. Instead of burying myself *outside*, I needed to bury myself *inside*.

I cleared out a room in our rental flat. My mates and I built a big wooden box inside the room. At the bottom of the box we placed an actual open coffin. Around and above the coffin we built another box so that I could sit up. We ordered about £800 worth of soil. I climbed into the coffin and my mates filled the big box with soil. Made a bit of a mess, to be fair. We didn't tell the landlord what we were doing.

Burying myself alive inside the flat was, of course, not quite the same as doing it outside. It did, however, allow me to test myself, to see if I could endure a full seven days in closed quarters, alone, with no food. It allowed me to fail or succeed on my own terms, without the mission being affected by external factors like the weather. Perhaps more importantly, though, it consolidated in my mind the idea that feats of endurance would always be subject to logistical difficulties. Success would depend on my ability to ignore those difficulties. To keep my mind focused on the end goal, and then deal with problems as and when they arose. There would surely always be a solution, but if I allowed myself to worry too much about the hurdles, I would never get past the first one.

I completed the seven days in that coffin. I suppose some people would be overcome by the claustrophobia. Not me. I found it a good environment to be alone with my thoughts. It was a bit like running in that way. Life had been busy, and this was an opportunity to slow down. I relished it. As I lay there – cramped, hungry, uncomfortable and alone – I had time to reflect. I'd clearly become in some way addicted to challenging myself. Maybe that addiction had replaced something that had left me when I kicked the gambling. Maybe, though, there was also something else going on. I'd left home at the age of 17, and the years that followed were difficult for me. I found life hard. My regular, day-to-day existence had felt like a struggle. The feats of endurance with which I had started to challenge myself, however, were in certain respects even tougher. They helped me to put normal life into perspective. Compared to running back-to-back ultramarathons, or pulling a car along the seafront in Worthing, or burying yourself alive for a week, normal life seemed kind of ... easy. These challenges made me feel, at some level, that ordinary life was good.

I emerged from that box after seven days unable to walk properly. I wobbled all over the place. The advice, when breaking your fast after several days, is to go easy on your stomach with small quantities of fruit and nuts. I ordered a large Domino's stuffed crust pizza and a can of Special Brew, which I followed up with £10 worth of my favourite pick 'n' mix. It didn't do wonders for my digestion. These effects soon wore off, though. Good thing too, because the following day I'd agreed to accompany a friend of mine on a three-day hike to the most remote pub in Scotland. After a week in a coffin, that hike was perhaps a little harder than it might otherwise have been, but we completed it without too much trouble.

• • •

Christmas came around. Emily had still not consented to go on a date with me. But I had still not given up hope.

My friends and I decided to do a Secret Santa. Our mutual friend rigged it so that I got Emily. That's what mates are for. I bought her two tickets to a comedy club in Brighton. As I presented the gift, I charmingly said: 'You can take me, if you like!' I guess she felt she couldn't refuse, and that was how I finally managed to persuade Emily to go on a date with me.

We started seeing each other a little bit more, but I'm sure I was a difficult person to be with. She was a practising Christian and I wasn't. Her attention was taken up by her little boy, mine by my slightly crazy feats of endurance. In the past, whenever I'd been in a relationship, the relationship would take second place to all my other plans. It would just have to slot in around my running. Emily wasn't having that. She was entirely supportive of everything I wanted to do. She encouraged me to follow my dreams. But she refused, quite rightly, to be an afterthought. That was not, she told me, the way things would work between us. If I wanted to be with her, I realised, I would have to learn to act differently in a relationship.

Which posed a bit of a problem, because by now I was searching for a new challenge. I'd started once more to look further afield, and the mission I had in mind would take me away from home – and from Emily – for a very long time ...

8

AFRICA GEEZER

I had spent a lot of time staring at a map of the world and considering the various land masses. My gaze kept returning to Australia. After the Asia to London run, my plan had been to attempt to run across Australia from west to east. The outback of central Australia could be brutal in terms of climate, but if I chose the correct time of year and timed my run to coincide with the Australian winter, I reckoned it would be do-able. It would be hot, for sure, and long – about 4,000 kilometres – but it probably wouldn't kill me.

When Covid happened and I had to take a year out, it meant that the plan to run Australia was put on hold. Even once the restrictions started to relax, the rules on travel remained complicated. And in any case, by this time another land mass was making eyes at me.

Africa.

My previous trip to the continent, when I'd visited Egypt and Kenya, had clearly affected me profoundly. It had been a formative journey. Before that I – like many Brits and other Europeans, I expect – had viewed Africa as one big homogenous place, no different in the north than the south, the east than the west. My trip to Egypt and Kenya, however, had quickly taught me that I was wrong about that. Even from my experience of those two countries, I could see that Africa was infinitely varied and completely different to anywhere else I was used to. I found myself thinking about it often, and longing to return. There's a phrase for it – *mal d'Afrique* – and somewhere at the back of my mind I always intended to attempt an African run after my Australian project. Now, circumstances were different and I realised that I preferred to ditch the idea of Australia and move straight to the continent that had so entranced me when I first visited it. I knew, after the Asia to London run, that I had the stamina and the endurance to run long distances day after day. As I stared at the map of Africa, I wondered if it was possible to run the entire length of the continent. Was that a thing that could be done? More importantly, was it a thing that could be done by me?

I didn't see why not.

I googled the northernmost point of Africa. Ras Angela is situated in northern Tunisia. I googled the southernmost point of Africa. Cape Agulhas is in the Western Cape of South Africa. I wondered if anybody had ever taken on the task of running between these two points. It would have been helpful if they had, because I'd have been able to learn something about how they'd achieved it. I searched extensively, however, and couldn't find any record of anybody having completed such a journey. I would be the first.

I figured that it would make best sense to run north to south rather than south to north. My reasoning was that it would be easier and cheaper to get all my stuff to Tunisia than to South Africa. All I'd need to do was drive my van down through Europe. So I then tried to work out the most direct route between Ras

Angela and Cape Agulhas. A crow would fly in a straight line down the spine of the continent. That route would take me through Tunisia itself, into Algeria, then through Niger, Nigeria, Cameroon, Congo, the Democratic Republic of Congo, Angola, Namibia and South Africa. With that route in mind, I spent some time trying to work out if there were any reasons why I *shouldn't* try to run this shortest distance between north and south. What was the political situation in each of these countries? What were the border restrictions? It was clear from my research that Algeria would present difficulties at the border, but I'd have to solve those somehow because the only other option would be Libya, where the complex and unstable political situation made it a much less attractive prospect. Yeah, Libya would be tricky, but so would Niger. The border between Algeria and Niger looked like it was very difficult to cross because it had a big problem with terrorism from Isis and Al-Qaeda groups, and significant humanitarian issues.

Already the most direct route was looking dicey. I moved my imaginary line to the west. Perhaps I could run through Algeria and into Mali. I quickly realised that would be a bad call, because Mali had troubles of its own. It saw frequent clashes between armed militia groups and even the involvement of the Russian mercenary unit the Wagner Group. I moved my line west again, from Mali to Mauritania. So far as I could tell, the border between Algeria and Mauritania was open to locals but difficult for tourists. Maybe it would be possible for me to cross it, though. It certainly looked like my best bet, because the border between Algeria and Morocco was also closed.

So the route through Mauritania, as far as I could tell, was the best of a bad bunch. It wouldn't be simple to get into that country, but there was a glimmer of hope. Once I was in Mauritania, I'd be in the extreme west of the continent. Therefore my only real option, if I still wanted to avoid Mali, was to follow the western coast of North Africa, through Senegal and Guinea. I noted that Guinea had recently had a coup, so things might be a bit dodgy there, but perhaps I could get through that country and into Côte d'Ivoire. I'd have to pass through Ghana, Togo and Benin before meeting up with my original straight line in Nigeria and Cameroon, and from there heading south. It would still mean passing through the Democratic Republic of Congo – a famously unstable country – but I could traverse it at its narrowest point and hopefully be in and out.

This was a much longer route than the straight line between Tunisia and South Africa – we were talking 15,000 kilometres, or the equivalent of 357 marathons – but the more research I did, the more I realised that I was at the mercy of the complicated political situations throughout the continent. I certainly didn't have the luxury of planning my route according to geography, topography or climate. If I had to run through desert, I'd have to run through desert. If I had to run through jungle, I'd have to run through jungle. Whatever the route threw at me, I'd have to deal with it. That was the mission.

I had no help with this initial research. It was just me and a phone. I made occasional use of web forums and read the comments of others who'd overlanded the continent by car. These were useful sources of information, but it soon became clear that

I was embarking on a unique mission. A few people had done stretches of ultra-running in northern Africa. Some desert marathons took place in Morocco, Egypt and Tunisia. The route that was forming in my mind, however, appeared to be untrodden in its entirety. This challenge was new.

The logistical intricacies of such a project took shape in my mind. At first, I imagined that it would be much like the Istanbul to London run, only longer. I could manage with the bare necessities of my rucksack and its scant contents. When I started zooming in on Google Earth, though, to examine the terrain through which I'd be running, it soon became clear that this was not a project I could undertake alone. There would be vast stretches of desert where I'd be running with no guarantee of seeing any other human for days or even weeks, and crucially nowhere to replenish my water supplies. This wasn't like running through Europe, where I could be pretty much certain of a petrol station every few miles, with its fresh water tap and a fridge full of sustaining sausage rolls. Running through Africa would be a completely different prospect. I'd need support of some kind.

My first thought was that I'd need a mate to drive the route with me, and a war chest of about £20,000. I calculated this figure on the back of an envelope, based on loose estimates of how much we would need to spend on essentials such as petrol, visas and food. I'd never had money, which meant I knew how hard it was to come by. That mentality enabled me to think as frugally as possible. Even £20,000 was not an accessible sum for me. The more I allowed it to increase, the more inaccessible the project as a whole would become.

I couldn't budget for expensive – or even inexpensive – hotel rooms or meals in restaurants. I couldn't even allow contingencies for things going wrong, for bribes or for vehicle breakdowns. I had to assume that everything would go according to plan.

Big assumption.

For a while, the concept of running the entire length of Africa stayed just that: a concept in my mind. As soon as I started actively working it out, though, I started to talk to people about it. The more I talked about it, the more my thoughts on financing the project evolved. I became friendly with a YouTuber called Zac. He'd built an entire career from his YouTube channel and he encouraged me to think differently about the financing. He suggested that instead of focusing on getting the job done for as little money as possible, I should think more creatively. If I could find a way to invest some more money upfront, I might then be able to turn the project into a business that ended up generating way more than I'd spent. This would make it an attractive proposition to those who might be interested in funding it.

I realised that it wasn't smart to make no financial provision for things going wrong, and that I would need more than one person in my support team. I allowed myself to think in terms of upping my budget from £20,000 to £40,000, and taking a three-person support team, so that we could film content along the way for YouTube and social media. Nobody would receive any wages, but the hope was that we would generate enough money to pay them at the end. Then I started having conversations with people who might be in a position to invest. A friend of a friend had made a few million in crypto. He was a Worthing lad who had heard about me and who was looking to invest in different projects. He liked the idea. Another friend of a friend was a professional footballer with a bit of money behind him. He was interested too. I realised that Zac was right, and that the way I was going to make this thing work was by getting sponsors who would put up the money that I needed in return for publicity on our YouTube and social media channels as and when the project gained traction. There was no point approaching brands to invest simply because they thought I was doing something admirable. Their motivation would be to get their products in front of eyeballs. If my expedition could provide a platform for my sponsors to do just that, my attempt to be the first person to run the entire length of Africa suddenly became much more viable.

The crypto guy ended up giving us £50,000. That was a massive moment. In return, I offered to give him £75,000 back and a 25 per cent profit share of anything else we made from sponsorship. I was still thinking in terms of the project costing no more than £40,000, so I figured we were pretty much covered for most of the mission. Then I met a documentary producer, who suggested we make a full-on documentary of the run.

I liked the idea and we started working together. The producer brought more people on board. He encouraged me to hire a project manager so that I didn't have to think about logistics – I only had to think about running. I did as he suggested. The team grew and grew, way past my initial conception of one guy with his rucksack pounding the trails of Africa, way past the stripped-down group I thought I could afford when I was thinking of running the project on a shoestring. Way past what I could actually afford. No matter, I was told. Part of the plan was that the production team would bring on big brand sponsors and sell the documentary to streaming platforms. In return, I'd have vastly more money to play with and carry out the mission properly. It sounded good at the time. I was all in.

• • •

The remit of my three-person team would be to produce content throughout the expedition, and do whatever else was required to help me get the mission done. In order to find these three people, I put out a message on Instagram to say that I was planning to run the length of Africa, and that I was looking for companions. 'This will probably be the most challenging and exhausting eight months of all our lives, but with the right team it'll also be the most exciting, fulfilling and life-changing.' I received a bunch of applications and whittled the hopefuls down to a shortlist of six. I invited the six down to Worthing for an interview. Not your regular kind of interview, though. I wasn't looking for people who were good with a spreadsheet. I was looking for people who could deal with the unexpected and work well as part of a team in unfamiliar environments and under pressure. I couldn't dump them in the middle of the Sahara Desert, of course, or test their ability to cope with a South African township environment. But I could definitely throw them some curveballs, and that's what I intended to do. I warned the interviewees that the process would take a couple of days, but they certainly had no idea what I had planned for them and I figured that was the way it should be.

On the appointed day, I picked them up from Worthing station and we drove straight to the pub. We had a pint together and a bit of a chat so I could get the measure of them. Then we all piled back in the van and I drove them out to the forest. I unloaded them, gave them a tent, told them I'd see them the next morning and drove off, leaving them to cope by themselves for the night. I picked them up the next morning and drove them to the running track. 'You've got two hours,' I said. 'Let's see how far you can run.'

The candidates dealt well with the unexpected. They impressed me. I couldn't take everyone, though. I had to make a choice and my first choice was Stan. In fact, Stan and I had met before. He'd been the cameraman who had documented the exploits of a mate of mine, Tom Davies, who had dribbled a football for 120 kilometres across England. I'd helped out as one of the pacemakers and Stan had run or walked about 100 kilometres of the route, having only ever run 10 kilometres before. It meant he had good experience with a camera, good experience with YouTube and also a bit of grit. I liked that.

My next choice was Harry. Originally from the UK, he had lived in Mexico and done some travelling in the Middle East. He spoke Spanish and told me that, if I gave him the job, he'd learn French. This would be a real advantage because we'd be travelling through a number of countries where French was spoken alongside other African languages. He also had a good working knowledge of cameras, so I came to the conclusion that he'd be a good guy to have along with us.

Olivia, an American from California, also had experience behind the camera. She had spent a year in Ghana with the Peace Corps, which trains and deploys volunteers to provide aid worldwide, so she knew what it was like to immerse yourself in the culture and reality of life in an African country. Crucially, I was mindful that I didn't want our project to be entirely male. Olivia's presence would bring female perspective to the project that I was keen to harness. I decided that she would be the third member of our team.

I explained to Stan, Harry and Olivia that I didn't yet have the money to pay them, but once we'd managed to raise the funds, I would back-pay their wages and also give them a share of any profits. They were happy with the risk and accepted the terms. It meant I had my team.

. . .

I planned to start running in November 2022. I was desperate for kick-off. And for a while, it looked like the plans of the production team were going to come good. They told me that a major TV network had offered us £180,000 for the rights to the content. I was buzzing. I couldn't believe that we were going to do this thing in a proper, legit way.

Then came the bad news. They wanted me to wait until February 2023. It was just about do-able weather-wise, although it would have meant spending the winter training in England before heading straight to the heat of Africa. More to the point, though, I just didn't want to wait. I'd been preparing for months and I was done with hanging around. The money, however, would mean that I could pay my team properly and the TV deal meant the whole expedition would make better sense for any sponsors. So I said okay.

November passed. December passed. Thinking there was money to cover it, I went to Gran Canaria to train. Here I could test myself in different environments. At sea level it would be hot and humid. But there were also hills so I could train at altitude. Importantly, the climate of the Canary Islands meant that the shock to the system when I arrived in Africa wouldn't be so great. I rented a little Airbnb and ran 30 to 40 kilometres a day. I also started paying out for other costs. We bought equipment. We got the van done up in preparation. But come January, the TV deal still hadn't been signed. The producer came to me and said he didn't think it was a good deal after all, that I shouldn't sign it. I hadn't managed to enthuse people enough. The sponsors we'd hoped for had failed to materialise, probably because most people thought I'd never complete the mission. The whole set-up was fizzling out. It soon became clear to me that I'd spent money I didn't have.

The people around me said I should continue to wait, so that we could have another go at raising funds and ensuring we had enough money at the very start of the project to complete it. But I was sick of waiting. I was sick of people's spiel with no results. I didn't really care about the money; I only cared about the mission. By this time, all I could think about was getting started. I remembered the realisation I'd come to as a result of my previous feats of endurance, that grand projects would always be subject to logistical difficulties. Success depended on my ability to focus on the end goal and deal with problems as and when they arose. Somewhere along the way I'd forgotten that. I was allowing logistics to delay me. If I continued to do so, the mission would never happen.

February arrived. I made the decision to ditch all the fancy production people who'd tried to make this a legitimate project. There would be no documentary. No £180,000. No sponsors, at least not at first. I would just start running with my team and the few quid that remained, and hope that we could deal with the issue of funding and sponsorship as we went along. My plan was still to raise funds for The Running Charity. To hell, though, with everything else. I just wanted to start tearing up the tarmac.

But then I received another blow.

The plan had always been to start in Tunisia and from there cross the border into Algeria. We were all set to move our gear to North Africa when word came through that Algeria had refused us a visa. Tunisia's only other border is with Libya, which was out for the reasons I'd already investigated. So without that Algerian visa, the mission would be over almost as soon as it had begun.

My plan was to run the length of Africa. It was looking impossible that I would be able to start it in Tunisia, so there was only one other option: to flip the whole expedition on its head and, instead of running north to south, to run south to north. This would give us more time to resolve the problem of getting into Algeria, perhaps by cooking up some mad little plan which we hadn't yet worked out. It would, however, mean running into the prevailing winds, rather than having the wind behind me. Not ideal, but I'd just have to live with it. Trouble was, getting the gear shipped out to South Africa rather than transporting it myself to Tunisia would cost all the money I had left, leaving me with nothing with which to start the mission.

At the very last minute, just before leaving the UK, I managed to arrange a meeting with a fundraising platform called Givestar. Through them, I secured just about enough to get us out to South Africa and on the road, but nowhere near enough to complete the whole run. I knew, though, that I could sit around waiting for years for the right moment.

Wasn't going to happen.

I decided we should just put the van on a boat and fly to South Africa.

9

SKINT GEEZER

The boat with the van left in February 2023. I decided we should go to South Africa as soon as possible. It would give us an opportunity to think about our route in a little more detail, and it would give me the opportunity to train in a warmer environment than the south coast of England in February. Just as importantly, it was actually cheaper for us to be in South Africa than it would have been to stay in the UK.

But this decision affected my girlfriend too, of course. Emily and I were not at all clear whether our relationship was going to survive the trip. As always, she championed me, but it would be wrong to suggest that, as my plans for the Africa run progressed, things didn't become a little strained. I was planning to be out of the country for a year. We had no idea what that meant for us or the relationship. We had no idea whether we would both feel the same way on my return. We said goodbye one night, just before she travelled to Canada to see her sister. Neither of us knew where our heads or our hearts would be when we met again.

Olivia and I flew to Cape Town. The boys – Stan and Harry – wanted to spend a little more time with their girlfriends before the start of the expedition. Olivia and I stayed in a hostel for a week.

And during that week, I began to have doubts about whether I'd made the right call about my team. Olivia didn't relish sleeping in a hostel. She seemed less relaxed than I was about going without something to eat for four or five hours, or about certain creature comforts not being readily available. These were perfectly normal characteristics. Olivia was no different to almost everybody else in these respects. The expedition on which we were about to embark, however, would require us to endure certain hardships. I wondered if Olivia would thrive in those circumstances.

When Stan and Harry joined us, we hired an Airbnb in Fish Hoek, a predominantly white part of Cape Town. I knew something of South Africa's history; I'd heard of the horrors of apartheid and racial segregation but I'd naïvely expected that segregation was a thing of the past. I could tell, almost as soon as we arrived in Cape Town, that to some extent it remained. Apartheid was no longer a government policy, of course, but the Black population and the white population remained quite separate. There were Black areas and there were white areas. If you walked into a bar, you could instantly tell if it was a white bar or a Black bar. The two populations remained distinct and – so far as I could tell – tended not to mix that much. From the moment we arrived, race felt like an ever-present issue in a way it didn't on the south coast of England.

The race issue made me uncomfortable in Cape Town. Back home, I felt insulated from racial differences. Perhaps that was just my privilege, but I'd never had to confront this issue in the same way. And it didn't bode well for the journey ahead – a journey during which almost everybody we met would be Black. I wanted no friction to exist on account of a difference in skin colour, but perhaps I was too hopeful. Perhaps my inbuilt assumption that I didn't see colour was not accurate. If so, I'd have to get over it, and quickly.

As well as running daily, I spent a lot of time at the gym in the lead-up to the mission. My workouts focused 50 per cent on strength training and 50 per cent on stretching and stabilisation work. I wanted to ensure that my knees and ankles and various stabilising muscles and ligaments in my legs were strong in order to prevent injury. I knew these parts of my body would get beaten up from nearly a year of running, so I wanted them to be in the best possible shape before I started. I also wanted to get a little bit bigger because I knew I would lose weight quickly once the mission commenced. If I was too small to start with, I'd be in trouble. I didn't follow any kind of scientific nutrition plan to bulk up – I just ate what I fancied and plenty of it, mostly from the hot food counter of a South African supermarket called Checkers. I'd have liked only to have focused on issues of fitness, suppleness and bulk, but, as I was quickly learning, an expedition such as this required me to consider matters other than my own physical wellbeing. For the first time, I found myself in the position of having to manage a team.

I'd never really been in any kind of leadership position. In all my jobs, I'd been at the bottom of the hierarchy. Running from Asia to London had been a solitary pursuit. Mates had helped me out in my subsequent endeavours, but never had I felt like I was any kind of a leader. The concept discomfited me from the very beginning. I had no desire to be anybody's boss. I didn't want to tell people what to do, any more than I wanted anybody else to tell me what to do. I wanted to empower the others to make their own decisions. Partly it was a character trait, partly I simply didn't want to be responsible for the morale and motivation of the team. These were most definitely my failings. The production team who'd been trying to persuade me to go for a TV deal had told me that I'd need a project manager to deal with the day-to-day logistics of the expedition, so that I could simply concentrate on the running. I'd disregarded that advice when we parted ways. Now I found myself having to be that project manager. My strengths did not lie in that area and it didn't take long for this uncomfortable truth to have an effect on the team dynamics.

I learned pretty quickly that I lack communication skills. Different people require different managerial styles in order to perform well, and I soon realised that I didn't know what buttons to press to encourage the best out of my team. Perhaps more importantly, my way of doing things is different to most others'. I felt certain that to achieve our ultimate goal, to get from our starting point to our final destination with the scant funds at our disposal, we would have to move fast. We couldn't be held up by worries. We couldn't let perfect be the enemy of good. We just had to start. It made me impatient, and when I encountered disagreement within the team regarding my approach and vision, it caused friction.

Had I been a skilled manager of people, I'd have known that the best way to align the team would have been to communicate my vision better. I failed to do that. I didn't know how.

The longer we spent in Cape Town, the more concerned I grew that Olivia was not the right person for my team. I felt that my personality would clash with hers, and without the management skills to rectify this situation, I couldn't see how the relationship could continue. It wouldn't be the right outcome for the project, it wouldn't be fair on the team and, as far as I could see, it wouldn't be fair on Olivia.

I knew that if I had to make a change, it had to be done quickly: now, while we were in Cape Town and before the mission itself had started. I wrestled with my conscience. Should I discuss my concerns with the guys? I decided not to. My rationale was that if *I* was about to be let go, I wouldn't want to think that people had been discussing this matter behind my back. It would be more respectful to Olivia to have the conversation with her first. So, one morning, I asked Olivia if we could have a private chat. I explained my concern that I didn't think this was going to work out. I told her how much I appreciated her enthusiasm for the project and everything she'd brought to the planning phase, and I meant it. But from now on, I'd decided to move forward with a different team. I told her I'd ensure she was paid for the time she'd put in, and that there would be some profit share at the end of the mission.

Olivia asked if we could discuss the matter with Harry and Stan. Her response confused me, but I said okay. We all sat in the lounge of our flat and I reiterated my thinking, and my decision that we were to move forward without Olivia. They took the news badly, especially Stan. He questioned my leadership skills. He threatened to leave. He, and the whole group, were very upset.

In the days that followed I tried to explain my reasoning. I knew what was coming. I knew that to run ultramarathons daily through gruelling, and potentially hostile, environments would require me to prioritise my own mental space. If I had concerns about the team, the whole mission was in jeopardy. I struggled to articulate these thoughts, and I think they struggled to understand them. The others saw this as being as much their mission as it was mine. They didn't feel I had the right to make the decision that I'd made. There's no doubt that they'd sacrificed a lot to be here, that they'd committed to the project all the way through the planning period during which I hadn't been able to pay them. They felt betrayed. I understood their position. It certainly wasn't a decision that I wanted to make, and perhaps I executed it poorly. I don't know.

In the end, Olivia left. It was a sad turn of events, and certainly not the outcome I would have chosen. Stan, Harry and I struggled to an agreement, but the dynamic remained strained. I was learning, even before the mission properly started, that leadership was a hell of a sight more difficult than I had predicted. I think that, in wanting to empower my team as much as possible so that I could concentrate solely on myself, I lost a certain amount of respect. I'd failed properly to establish that I was in charge. This balance between empowering a team and commanding respect lies at the heart of good leadership. I realised I would have to get a lot better at it. And I realised that if I was successfully going to run the entire length of Africa, I wouldn't only be required to demonstrate my physical fitness. Feats of endurance such as this required other skills, and I wasn't sure that I had them.

• • •

With Olivia gone, we needed to reassign the responsibilities within the group. Stan's main responsibility, as it always had been, was video editing. He was to concentrate on creating the videos for our regular YouTube updates. Critical work, since we had insufficient money and would need to attract the interest of sponsors quickly once we'd started. Harry was also there because of his skill behind the camera, but I asked him to shift his focus to logistics. And since we were now one person down, we had another position to fill.

We posted on a Facebook page called Overlanding Africa. It catered to a community of people who had either overlanded Africa in the past, or intended to do so. We received interest from several applicants, but one guy stood out. His name was Jarred, and he was a South African with good film experience. He agreed to join us, and so we were a four-person team again.

We collected our van when the boat arrived. It was the Iveco – formerly a school minibus – that I had used to take people on adventures to Scotland and Wales. I'd converted it to make it a suitable support vehicle on a journey through Africa. Our priorities were to ensure we had a means of charging our equipment, somewhere to sleep, and a way of carrying water. We fitted solar panels and installed big batteries, so that we could charge our phones, laptops and cameras. We installed two sets of bunk beds. There was no plumbing, but we figured we could carry about 400 litres of water at any one time, in 25-litre jerrycans. The water was heavy, which we knew would affect our petrol consumption, but without water there was no mission. The van had no cooking facilities, so we would have to use a camping hob for hot meals.

We moved from Cape Town a couple of days before our start date. It felt good to leave that town behind, partly because I was keen for the mission to start, partly because things had been difficult there. We drove south to Cape Agulhas, Africa's southernmost point. Situated in the Overberg region, and overlooked by a red-and-white striped lighthouse, Cape Agulhas is a beautiful little countryside town on whose shores the Atlantic Ocean meets the Indian Ocean. I stood at that point and looked out over the choppy seas. I almost felt I could be standing on the Scottish coast. Then I turned 180 degrees to look north. In that direction, many thousands of kilometres away, lay my destination: Ras Angela in Tunisia. I tried not to think too hard about the places, or the paces, in between.

We camped in the van for the first time, about a kilometre from the start point. The top bunks were the worst, but I thought it would be good for morale if I took one of them. I'd be spending a lot of time in that bunk, sleeping at night and recuperating after my daily runs, but if my biggest worry was which mattress I'd be crashing on, I was probably not cut out for the wider task at hand. So I lay on that top bunk on the evening of 21 April 2023, the night before the mission started, and thought about what lay ahead.

Ultrarunning is not like many other sports, where success depends on your individual performance at a particular moment.

The shot at goal in football. The perfect tackle in rugby. The birdie in golf. For me, there was no distinct moment to get nervous about. I didn't really doubt my fitness or my mental ability to complete the task. Any nerves I felt centred around the hope that I didn't get injured quickly. That would be the bummer. I didn't plan to ease myself in slowly. I intended to start off with a succession of 50-kilometre days. I'd never repeatedly done that kind of distance, not even during the Asia to London run. I wasn't naïve enough to think that my body wouldn't encounter the stresses and strains any machine might expect through excessive daily use. But to sustain an injury immediately, in the first few days, would be embarrassing. I felt reasonably confident, but there was definitely an element of the unknown and I hoped that my body would hold out.

I had other anxieties too. The tensions in the group still bubbled under the surface. Even more importantly, I knew we barely had enough money to last a few weeks. Our only real hope of raising more money was through brand sponsorship, and we'd only get that if brands thought we were a good vehicle to raise awareness of their products. We'd only be of interest to them once they saw what we were doing – that this wasn't just an aspiration, it was a real-life endeavour. So we had to start the mission before we had any hope of raising money. I had faith in my plan – to me it was a no-brainer that we should just start the run with whatever money we had – but I knew it was a high-risk strategy. If we failed to pique the interest of brands and sponsors along the way, the mission would fail not for reasons of fitness, injury or personal relationships. We'd simply run out of cash. Not only would I have to stop running, I wouldn't be able to pay the boys the money I'd promised them. I wouldn't even have the funds to get home. The pressure I felt about the money issue was intense – like the pressure I felt when I was gambling, but worse because other people's livelihoods were at stake.

Mostly, though, I was excited. I'd been talking about this project for a long time. I was ready to start delivering. The task was huge, but in my head it was simply a sequence of many smaller tasks. My job the following day was to run 50 kilometres. I didn't need to think about anything else. I'd worry about day two the following evening. A journey of a thousand miles begins with a single step. I was ready to take that step.

• • •

I managed a few hours' sleep that night, and woke early the next morning. It was still dark and cold outside with a light rain. I pulled a jumper and a jacket over my running gear, and put on one of the 25 pairs of trainers I'd brought with me. Then we drove to our start point.

The bright beam of the lighthouse flashed its warning across the headland. White surf rolled in from the south through the grey dawn. It was just the four of us: me, Stan, Harry and Jarred. The eyes of the world were not on us. Hardly anybody knew what we were about to undertake. It was Jarred's idea that I should fill a small bottle of seawater from that choppy southern coast and carry it the full length of Africa, where I would deposit it back into the Mediterranean on the northern coast of Tunisia. I clambered over the rocks to the edge of that ocean and performed that little ritual. Then I turned my back on the sea and faced north. The time had come to start.

So I started.

10

CRAZY
GEEZER

As soon as I began running on that first day, I was buzzing. This moment had been a long time coming. I'd originally wanted to be on the road six months earlier, but it wasn't just that my impatience had been satisfied. I felt as though my entire life had been leading up to this moment. More so than anything I'd done before, it was this journey that would allow me to prove what I was made of.

These were the rules. I would run as far as possible each day. The guys would meet me in the van at regular intervals of about 20 kilometres so I could rest, refuel and rehydrate. While I was running, they would go about their various logistical and video-editing tasks. At the end of each day we would drive somewhere to camp or – if possible – to sleep in a lodge or hotel. The next morning, we'd return to the point at which I'd stopped running, and do it all again. Rinse and repeat for 15,000 kilometres, without taking a single day off.

We had our rough route through South Africa planned out. Through most of the country – and indeed through most of Africa – there would be a single highway that I needed to follow. There were very few directions, very few side roads or diversions. It was simply a case of facing forwards and running the same road for the whole day, or even on occasion for weeks at a time. Each evening I would zoom in on the route and calculate a run of 50 or 60 kilometres, and we'd plan our stopping point for the next evening. When I set out in the morning, I'd remain in touch with the team and they'd let me know where they'd meet me with the van for the stopping points along the way.

The sky was overcast that first day, the terrain an expanse of dry grass with mountains on the horizon. From time to time I stopped to rest and refuel. I wore a hydration vest which held two litres of water in a pouch with a straw attached so I could drink on the go. I would sip little and often rather than taking big swigs of water that would only make me want to pee. Inside the rucksack, along with my passport and phone, was a small sack filled with dried fruit and peanuts – high-energy snacks with a good variety of fats, protein and carbs to keep my energy levels up – and some sachets of salt and sugar that I could add to the water to help rehydrate me and replace lost electrolytes. I also carried with me a packet of biodegradable wet wipes, for the moment when nature came calling. And it didn't take long, as I headed north from Cape Agulhas, for me to feel the urge to perform what would become something of a ritual: my daily poo.

Nobody wants to run a marathon with full bowels. When I was in good health, this ritual would happen once or twice a day, depending on how much food I'd eaten to keep me going. There was no hope, of course, of finding a toilet. It was simply a matter of finding a suitable place to do my business – normally behind a bush, and out of sight of any locals, especially children. In the

UK, if the need ever took me to answer a call of nature, I'd have to check for brambles or stingers before making the old squat. Out here, I was a little more diligent. I didn't want to disturb any snakes, spiders or other creepy crawlies, and I certainly didn't want them to disturb me as I was in that delicately vulnerable position.

With the call of nature answered, I continued running. As I ran, I tried to problem-solve the overwhelming issue of money. We had started to make content for YouTube and Instagram, but we had to work out how best to present it to unlock the funding that we were going to need. I had vague ideas about how to do this, but at the moment it felt like a picture that was out of focus. Those long, solitary miles gave me the headspace I needed to gain some clarity. They gave me, as they always do, space to think.

I felt pretty good by the end of the first day. A bit stiff, perhaps, but that was to be expected. I filled a little bucket with water from one of the jerrycans and washed off the day's sweat and dust. Washing was not such a priority for the others, as they hadn't been running all day. In general, they would wait for those evenings when we stayed in a hotel to shower properly. Despite the tensions we'd encountered, there was a real sense of excitement among the team as we sat around and ate dinner that night. It was good to be on the go. The guys lit a barbecue and cooked some food. In general life, I'm not one to stick to regular mealtimes. Breakfast, lunch and dinner don't mean much to me. When I was running, they meant even less. I needed to eat all the time, so while the rest of the team would cook and eat dinner together, I'd stick to my standard diet of nuts, dried fruit, biltong and whatever snacks we could find from supermarkets and petrol stations along the way. If I wasn't running, I was either eating or resting.

The first day had been relatively straightforward from a running point of view. On Day 2, things changed. A small mountain range lies east to west across the southern tip of South Africa. I hadn't given the topography of the terrain too much thought. I'd looked briefly at the terrain and seen that I'd have to cross a few mountain ranges on my journey north, but I hadn't examined them in detail or thought too deeply about the challenges they might present. This wasn't carelessness on my part. Partly my mind was taken up with more important matters, such as funding. Partly it was an active decision not to get too hung up on the smaller details of the project, to keep the bigger picture firmly fixed in my mind, and to deal with any obstacles as and when they occurred. I couldn't sweat the small stuff, because if I did I'd never have even begun.

That mountain range was our first obstacle. We couldn't go round it. We had to cross it. That, along with the headwinds that came with our new trajectory of south to north, meant that the days that followed were hard running. I had no option but to endure the discomfort and push on through. At this early stage, my body was in decent nick, so I didn't allow myself to slow down and take it easier when the incline became steeper. Later in the run, of course, when my body was more pieced up, I'd have to approach hills differently. Early doors, I tried to pretend they didn't even exist and just kept going (although I do remember thinking on day two that if the rest of the mission was like this, I'd be in trouble ...)

I felt my body stiffen up a lot in those early days. It became harder to move from the hips down, and painful. Not a sharp, agonising, punch-in-the-face kind of pain, but a dull, ever-present ache as everything seized up. My body was not used to the punishment I was giving it. My knees and ankles became inflamed as I ran. At night I'd smear them with ibuprofen gel to numb the pain and reduce the inflammation, and they'd go down a bit. Sometimes I'd try to massage the blood out of my legs with baby oil, to help acclimatise my body to the hammering I was giving it. Muscle cramps would hit me at night. The bulk I'd acquired in Cape Town fell away very quickly – within a month I lost seven kilos of weight. Blisters stung my feet. There was no way I'd let them interfere with my running, no matter how painful they might be, but they did require some management. At the end of each day I'd wash my feet well in order to guard against infections that might enter my bloodstream through broken skin. Then I'd examine the blisters. I've developed, over my years of running, the ability to sense whether or not a blister is ready to be popped. If the skin under the surface still looks raw and the blister itself remains tough, it's best to leave it. If the blister bulges and is full of 'juice', it's probably time to give it a pop. I'd squeeze out all the transparent liquid, then wash it well and let it air-dry and harden overnight. A clean sock and I'd be ready to run on it again. I'm not saying it wouldn't sting, but I had bigger issues to think about than a little discomfort on the sole of my foot. It wasn't the only part of me that hurt, and it wasn't the worst.

Three days in, we were offered the opportunity to camp in a vineyard and make use of a hot shower and a proper toilet. I smile when I look back and think about how pathetically grateful we were to have that shower. It's a reminder of what an early stage we were at in the mission, and how green we were. Three days of roughing it felt substantial. Times were approaching, however, when we would go for several weeks without a hot shower or even the promise of one. Times were approaching when creature comforts would be scarce. We didn't know it then, but still: that accommodation and shower meant a great deal.

If that hot shower was a high point of the early days, the breakdown of our support vehicle was a definite low point. That vehicle was such a crucial part of the operation. It carried all our gear. It gave us a place to sleep. Most importantly, it meant the guys could meet me at regular intervals throughout the day so that I could refill the water in my hydration vest. The two litres that my water bladder carried was nothing like enough to hydrate me through 50 or 60 kilometres of running.

So when, five days in, the handbrake failed on the truck, it was a problem.

The guys had to drive all the way to Stellenbosch to find a repair shop. From there they needed to travel back to Cape Town to pick up a document for the van, leaving me without a support vehicle. It meant I had to carry full bottles of water with me, as well as enough food to last me. It was a rough day. A long, hot day when I ran out of water and the miles passed slowly. A day to put behind you. The guys managed to get the van fixed and to meet me at the end point. The following day brought torrential rain. I stepped out into it to start the marathon, and the guys took the van back to the repair shop for a second time. A mechanic there had offered to reinforce the windows in case anybody tried to smash them in from the outside. A very real possibility in South Africa, as I would soon find out.

This was an interesting country to run through, with its varied infrastructure and scenery. Every four or five days we'd allow ourselves a night in a cheap hotel. It was not like staying in the Ritz, but nor were these hotels like the place in Kenya where I'd been offered a bucket of water instead of a shower. They were much closer to European standards. I'd pass well-developed towns that almost *looked* European. I'd run through terrain that resembled the wine-growing regions of France.

And then, of course, I'd run through the townships.

The townships in South Africa are underdeveloped urban areas characterised by racial segregation. During the apartheid era they were specifically reserved for the non-white population. Today, the word 'township' has a specific legal meaning that is unrelated to race, but in practice these are grindingly poor Black areas. They are run down, slum-like and sketchy, especially for a solitary white dude like me.

I ran through my first township early in the run. It was nearing the end of the day and I was running uphill when the suburban sprawl appeared up ahead. I could tell just by looking at it that this was a poor area. The buildings were nothing more than broken sheds with corrugated tin roofs. There was no tarmac on the roads, just dirt. Any cars in the vicinity were old and beaten up. Rubbish littered the streets and spaghetti-like messes of cabling stole electricity from overhead pylons. People in ragged clothing sat on the side of the road holding up ten-rand notes in order to hitch a lift to the next town. I couldn't help but compare it to the predominantly white areas I'd seen up till now, where Porsches were parked in front of big houses with manicured lawns. I was aware that, thanks to the colour of my skin, it would be easy to mistake me for one of the wealthy Afrikaaners who lived in those big rich houses. It would be easy to come to the wrong conclusion. I understood how it might happen – I remembered being a skint kid in Worthing and dissing anyone I thought of as being rich or upper class. Something similar was happening here, but to a more extreme scale (I wasn't living under a tin roof) and with the complexity of racial politics baked in (I looked the same as the rich bastards).

So, all in all, I couldn't help but feel a little threatened by the environment. I'd heard stories about the townships. I'd heard of the extremes to which the terrible poverty sometimes drove its inhabitants. I knew there were places in some of the townships where you'd be stabbed for 5 rand, or about 20 pence. People had told me this, and they weren't joking. Now, as I ran through my first township, I felt the hot stare of strangers. Some were just curious. Others looked at me like I was a gazelle and they were a lion. It was a strange new environment for me, and I'll be honest: the township felt like a place where I shouldn't be. The vibe was more hostile than I expected. I decided on a strategy as I ran. I would make a particular effort to look stern. I'd frown and allow my eyes to express a hard glint. As soon as I made eye contact with anybody, however, I'd give them a big smile and appear super happy, before reverting to my original Hardest Geezer demeanour. I wanted everybody I passed to think I was friendly, but serious.

And sometimes I did make friends. In my first week I saw, running up ahead, a young Black man, maybe 16 years of age. He was fast. Faster than me. He stopped to stretch and I caught up with him. We ran together for a few kilometres and he told me how he wanted to be a rugby player and he was trying to get his fitness up for the rugby season. I guess he saw it as his way out of the townships. None of his mates wanted to come running with him, though, so here he was, smashing it up. He reminded me of myself, in a way. He also reminded me that the townships were not only populated by people out to rob us. Mostly they were populated by friendly, ordinary guys like this.

Not all my encounters were so inspiring, however. I was running through another township one evening and it had just got dark. I was 50 kilometres in and beginning to flag when, from nowhere, a guy sprinted up to me. It made me jump, and I immediately knew that this was not a good situation. The guy started running in front of me – close, about a metre away – and I became aware that there was a second guy running a little further behind me. We ran, in this awkward convoy, for maybe 30 seconds. My brain turned over as I tried to work out what was happening. They intended to rob me, of that I felt pretty sure. The situation was weird, though. If they meant to rob me, why hadn't they done so immediately? Why were they running with me? Why were they hesitating? I guessed that they were trying to suss me out. To assess the threat I posed to them. They lacked confidence in their ability to do the job. So I thought to myself: *If they're looking for a reason not to rob me, I'd better give them one.*

My strategy was simple: act like a crazy geezer. I picked up the pace and I started to yell. 'We're running! *We're running!*' I beat my chest, made my eyes wild and hollered into the night. 'Yes, brother! *YES!*' I jumped up and down. I shouted on the spot and made huge, exaggerated movements with my arms and legs. I acted reckless and unpredictable. Picking up the pace, I started running again, still shouting, roaring. 'Let's go faster! *Faster! FASTER!*'

I continued like this for a couple of minutes, and I could tell that the strategy was working. The wannabe robbers were freaked out by the crazy behaviour of this orange-bearded nutcase running along the road. The guy behind dropped back. The two guys started talking in a language I couldn't understand. Zulu, maybe, or Xhosa. I didn't understand their words, but I think I understood the tone of their conversation. The guy in front was up for it, whereas the guy behind clearly didn't have the stomach for the encounter. After a couple more minutes, the guy behind dropped off and we left him standing in the darkness.

The front guy was still with me, though. Still running. Still a threat. I noticed that he was carrying something in his hand. A toothbrush, maybe? I didn't like the look of it. I'd been a prison officer. I'd seen the kind of weapon that could be fashioned from a toothbrush and a razor blade, and now I looked more closely I thought I could make out a blade-shaped silhouette protruding from the shaft. I was pretty certain he wasn't there to offer me a shave and a hot flannel. I might have scared off one of my potential assailants, but this guy could still do me a lot of damage with his shiv.

So I continued in the same vein, sporadically shouting, occasionally grabbing him on the shoulder, giving him reason to think I was unpredictable and therefore not an easy target. 'I'm a warrior!' I yelled. 'Let's go faster!' I increasingly believed that he was not a proper gangster, a hardened criminal who would hit me hard, mess me up and rob me for everything I had without a moment's thought. I started acting a bit more friendly as we continued to run. Little by little I sensed the hostility ebb away from the encounter. We had reached the very outskirts of the township by now, so I eased off the crazy-geezer act and we started talking a little more normally.

'My friend was going to rob you,' the guy said.

'Okay,' I replied. In a weird way, it was a relief to hear that. I hadn't been inventing dangers, and his admission implied that he no longer meant me any harm. No doubt I still sounded a bit wary, however. The shiv remained in his fist, after all. 'But you're not going to rob me, are you? We're brothers, right?'

He nodded. 'God wouldn't like it if I robbed you,' he said.

'You're right about that, brother. My friends are coming soon anyway. They're on their way. They'll be here in a minute. We can get you some food and stuff, if you like.'

'That's what I'm doing,' he said. 'Trying to get food for my wife and family.'

All of a sudden, the vibe had changed. We chatted normally. He told me about life in the township. It upset him that there was no school for his children to attend. They lived a rough, hard life. It occurred to me that this might just be a sob story. If he couldn't rob me, maybe he could fleece me in another way. I didn't really think that was the case, though. I'd seen the townships, and his words had the ring of truth.

Eventually, the guys turned up. They didn't have the van with them. A rock had hit and shattered the windscreen so they had to get it fixed. A white South African guy had driven them to come and collect me. It meant they didn't have any food to offer my new acquaintance. No matter. We were friendly now. The shiv had disappeared and he was happy just to receive a lift back into the township. As we dropped him off by the side of the road, he said, 'God bless you.' Then he disappeared into the night.

The encounter shook me up. I knew there could easily have been a very different outcome. And although I knew at some level that I should expect nervy confrontations like that, it's not until you experience them that you learn how you're going to react. As we drove away from the township, it occurred to me that my road-side encounter had not been so different to the situations in which I'd found myself when I was working in the prison. The environments were completely different, of course, but in prison there had often been similar moments that, mishandled, could have gone south very quickly. I'd learned back then that there were different plays for different situations. To act dominant was often a reckless option. It could get you killed. Mostly, submissiveness was the safest choice. Give the aggressor what they want. Avoid violence. De-escalate. I'd been in enough situations, though, to realise that on occasion you could risk the dominant move. My time in a British prison had enabled me to make that judgement in a South African township, to see the situation for what it was rather than be blinded by its intensity.

I didn't realise it at the time, but there would be moments when my instincts would lead me to make a different choice. When the call to be dominant would likely lead to my death. For now, though, I was pleased that the episode was behind us. I'd safely negotiated a dangerous moment, and the mission could continue.

11

THIRSTY GEEZER

Running gives you time and space to think. It simplifies matters. It helps you strip away what is unimportant, and focus on what is necessary.

As I continued my journey north through South Africa, I spoke to Emily every day, sometimes for hours on end. Emily was, and is, religious. I had grown up an atheist and, as a teenager and young man, would definitely have mocked the idea that traditional wisdoms had anything to offer me. Surely they were nonsensical in the modern world, and out of date. My outlook was changing, however. Partly that was Emily's influence. I admired her values and it was not lost on me that she seemed prepared to wait for me as I pursued my mission, no matter how long it took. Emily would call herself a Christian, and her faith clearly provided her with a strong foundation. I did not consider myself a Christian, but I was beginning to see how some of those values could be beneficial to me in my life. The more I ran, the more we spoke and the more time I spent in my own head, the more I found myself entertaining these spiritual thoughts.

Of course, we also had to consider more mundane matters. My encounter in the township had reminded us that plenty of locals would see us as targets: white boys with a big van, food and a load of camera equipment. As we headed north, we could expect this to be a bigger deal. White people would be reasonably common in Namibia, but as we hit Angola and the Democratic Republic of the Congo, we would become more of a curiosity and therefore more of a target. People we spoke to along the way warned us especially about the dangers of the DRC – a war-torn country where poverty was endemic and violence rife. Our van was emblazoned with 'Project Africa' stickers. There wasn't a great deal we could do to stop ourselves looking like bait, but we decided that removing these stickers would make us look less like a bunch of white boys driving across Africa, asking to be robbed. So that's what we did.

And I had my mind on money too. Funds were dwindling and the importance of attracting sponsorship was still at the front of my thoughts. It was only as we approached the Namibian border that our fortunes changed.

A year before the run began, when I was trying to raise funds for the expedition, I messaged the *Dragon's Den* entrepreneur Steven Bartlett. I sent him a full pitch in my attempt to persuade him to invest, but he didn't see the message. A couple of weeks into the run, however, as the project started to gain some traction on social media through our YouTube updates and Instagram posts, he contacted me. 'Love what you're doing,' the message said. 'Is there a way I can still help?'

It was a turning point in the mission. I knew that Steven was associated with lots of different brands, so I messaged him back explaining the predicament: that we didn't have enough money to complete the mission, and could he put us in touch with brands who might be interested in sponsoring us? Turned out he could. Through Steven we signed sponsorship deals with PerfectTed and Huel, and all of a sudden everything changed. I could pay the guys, and we had funds to continue the journey. As soon as I signed those deals, the team dynamic improved. A weight had been lifted. I realised that it hadn't just been me who had been stressed out by the lack of funds. We all had. Now that the next few months looked slightly less precarious, we could all relax a little bit and focus on what was important: the mission.

• • •

The terrain and climate changed as we got closer to Namibia. With the hills behind us, our surroundings became less green and more desert-like. The air became drier, the sun more intense and the temperature increased. I tried not to think too hard about the impact this would have on my running. I knew there would be worse to come, so I just had to get on with it. I found myself drinking more water and slapped on some more factor 50 sunscreen, my complexion not being entirely suited to strong sun. I managed to keep my face, arms and legs protected, but I never managed to stop my hands becoming burned and blistered. I ran with closed fists, so the backs of my hands were always in direct sunlight, and sweating. To this day you can see scars on my skin from the sun damage. I refused to let these minor inconveniences and the change in the environment distract me from the job at hand: running. I felt tenacious and energetic, excited to be on the road and – despite the hitches we'd encountered along the way – pleased with our progress. Our numbers on social media started massively increasing. Our mission clearly interested people, and word of what we were trying to achieve had started to spread.

I ran faster on my last day in South Africa – Day 16 – than on any previous day. There had been tough days and tough moments, but good things lie on the far side of the struggle, and I felt stronger and more enthusiastic than at any point previously. Which was positive, because as the Namibian border approached, so did a new challenge. The lads had still not managed to repair the windscreen. This was a problem because we wouldn't be allowed to cross the border with smashed glass. Also, Jarred had a holiday booked, so we needed to take him to the airport on Day 17. All this was going to take time to sort out, but I didn't want to take a rest day. The only solution was for me to start running late on Day 17, cross the border by myself, and keep running in the Namibian desert until the guys caught up with me. It meant I could be running alone for up to 24 hours.

So I was enthusiastic but I was also nervous. This would be my first border crossing in Africa and I didn't know what to expect other than barren desert on the Namibian side. It would be cold at night and I wasn't certain what kind of nocturnal wildlife awaited in the desert. I didn't want to run blindly into lion territory, so I googled it. No lions, but the chance of big cats for sure. Before I even tackled the desert, though, I'd have to negotiate the border town. I'd heard that the towns on either side of the border were rough. Locals advised us not to be in these places by yourself, and especially at night. With the incident in the township fresh in my mind, this felt like a rogue move.

I arrived alone in the middle of the night at the South African side of the border crossing: a small collection of municipal buildings, and nobody about other than a handful of border guards. I was wearing my running gear and a head torch, and carried with me nothing but my passport and the contents of my rucksack: a tray of sausage rolls, a slab of Dairy Milk, some sweets and some wet wipes. Enough food, I hoped, to sustain me until the guys managed to pick me up. The border guards stamped my passport and I attracted a few strange looks. But only a few. No doubt they'd seen plenty of weird people pass this border in their time. They didn't seem very interested in me. I walked along a dark stretch of no man's land to the Namibian border, where I encountered a fresh set of officials. They looked me up and down. 'Where's your car?' one of them said.

I thought about explaining to them that I was running the length of Africa. Some people were able to understand that as a concept. Others weren't. I sensed that these guys would fall into the latter camp, so I simply said: 'I'm running into the desert. My friends are going to come and meet me later.'

They looked at each other. Then they looked at me. Then they shook their heads. 'No way,' the guy said. 'It's too dangerous. Don't do that.'

They didn't want me walking around the border town by myself late at night. They certainly didn't want me venturing unaccompanied into the desert. They explained to me that there was a hotel a kilometre down the road, and that I should stay there for the night. 'Okay,' I said with big smile. They entered the address of the hotel on the border form I had to fill out, and stamped my passport.

I was through.

By now it was one o'clock in the morning. With the border post behind me, I switched off my head torch. The border guards had freaked me out a bit, and I didn't want the light to draw attention my way. I started running. I had no intention of staying in the hotel, of course. My plan was to get through the border town as quickly as possible, and into the desert where I would at least be free of the threat of hostile humans, if not hostile animals. After a couple of minutes, however, I saw the silhouette of four guys standing in the road up ahead, perhaps 600 metres away. I stopped and squinted at them through the darkness. My heart started thumping. I knew what was coming. I was about to get robbed. No question about it. Why else would four geezers be blocking the road at that time of night? There was no beating my chest and acting like a crazy geezer to get out of this one. Turning back was out of the question, though. So I continued my approach.

As I drew near, the four guys simply wandered away. They disappeared into the night. It made no sense to me. What would they be doing there in the middle of a deserted road in the dead of night, if not looking for someone to hit? Sometimes you just have to thank your good luck. I picked up my pace and followed the road through the town and into the desert.

The temperature had dropped dramatically. It was freezing cold and I couldn't see very much at all, even though I'd put my

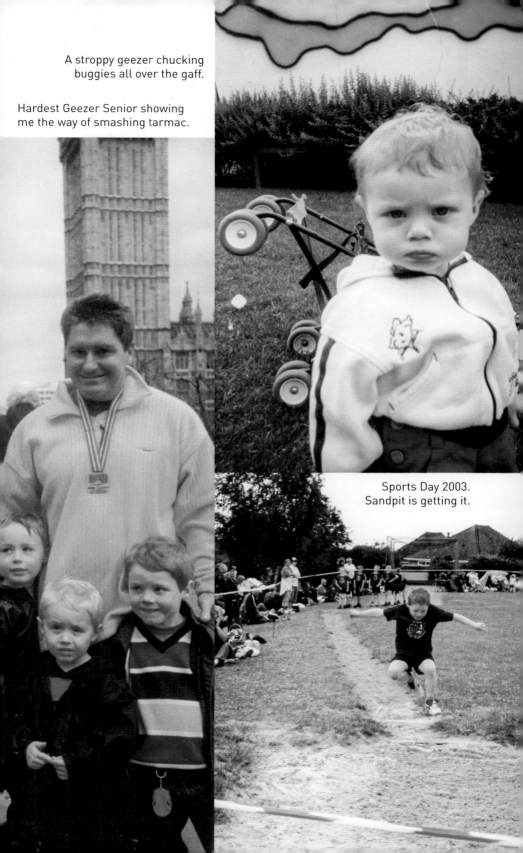

A stroppy geezer chucking buggies all over the gaff.

Hardest Geezer Senior showing me the way of smashing tarmac.

Sports Day 2003. Sandpit is getting it.

Becks wannabe. The grass wasn't so neat once we'd finished tearing it up.

Worthing Dynamos – hard geezers to a man.

20 June 2019. Setting off from Istanbul on my first back-to-back marathon.

Made it back to London 66 days later. I ran it in with The Running Charity, who I'd been fundraising for.

Digging my own grave – just before my first attempt at burying myself alive.

The southernmost tip of Africa. Minus one day from the start of the mission.

INDIAN OCEAN | ATLANTIC OCEAN

Worst boy band ever. The original team – Jarred, Stan, me and Harry.

With a township geezer who pounded the tarmac with me.

Me and Guus keeping it civilised in the Congo.

Chewing sand, breakfast, lunch and dinner.

Putting some Mauritanian kids through a football training session, Worthing United style.

Front of the pack on the final day. Tarmac didn't stand a chance.

Looking good, lads – beard game stronger than Gandalf.

And after all that, I came second.

head torch back on now I was away from the town. From time to time the moon would peek from behind the clouds, and now and then some starlight would appear. My sight, though, was not my most stimulated sense. My hearing was. I could hear things all around. Sinister rustlings. The sound of movement. Back in South Africa, I'd zoomed into my route on Google Maps and examined satellite imagery of southern Namibia. It looked empty. There were few human settlements but that didn't mean there wasn't life teeming all around me. I tried hard not to think too much of the big cats that might be in the vicinity. I tried hard not to imagine what might be out there. My head torch shone into the darkness, however, and occasionally I'd see the glint of light reflecting back from pairs of eyes in the desert terrain to my left and right. I don't know what made my heart pump more: the thought of being robbed at the border town, or the thought of what might be out there watching me run. If I met trouble, there was nobody in the vicinity to help. Not a single vehicle passed me that night. I felt very alone. Vulnerable. Scared.

It was an extremely long night.

All nights end, though. The main road through Namibia – the B1 – follows a northeasterly direction at first, so the sun rose almost in front of me, flooding the Namibian desert with its orange and pink light. It was a magnificent sight to witness all alone. I took my first proper look at the desert terrain of this new country. Dry, rocky ground surrounded me. Here and there, scrubby bushes tried to sprout through the hard-baked terrain. The road itself was narrow, with no hard shoulder. Cars remained infrequent.

I continued to run all morning, stopping only occasionally for water or food breaks, which entailed five or ten minutes by the side of the road. The temperature increased as the morning wore on. As midday approached, I started to flag. I'd been running almost non-stop since the border, rationing my water carefully because I didn't know how long it would take for the guys to reach me. I slowed down and started to walk through the pounding heat of the desert at midday. Deciding I needed to take a rest, I sat down on my rucksack by the side of the road.

My water pouch exploded.

What remained of my precious water sluiced out onto the desert ground, which quickly consumed it.

Great. Now I was alone in the desert in the hottest part of the day, with no water.

I carried on walking. Then I started to get dizzy from heat, dehydration and over-exertion. My body was giving up. I sat at the side of the road and tried to keep a clear head. Not easy. I was delirious. It looked like the border guards had been right: the Namibian desert was not a place to try to cross solo. More than anything else I needed water. There was none to be found, here in the middle of nowhere. My only hope was that a friendly car would pass and help me out. I sat by the side of the road and stuck out my thumb. I didn't hold out much hope. Even during the day, cars were a rare sight on this stretch of road. Eventually, though, I saw a vehicle approach from the south, its headlamps shimmering and bumping in the heat haze. The pick-up truck drew close but it didn't stop. Not immediately. It drove past, the driver staring curiously at me through the window. It then came to a halt, did a U-turn and repeated its drive past, the driver scoping me out for a second time. Stopped again.

The driver leaned out of the window of the pick-up and, rightly assuming that I spoke English, called out: 'Are you okay?'

I staggered to my feet, aware of the need to persuade him that I wasn't some crackhead looking for a mark to rob. I approached and, with a weak voice, said: 'I'm trying to run the length of Africa. I've run out of water and I need to get to the next town. Can I grab a lift?'

He thought about it for a moment, then nodded. 'No worries,' he said.

I climbed into the back of the pick-up and he gave me a bottle of water, probably the best water I'd ever drunk in my life. I stopped my Garmin watch so I knew which point I had to return to in order to continue the run, and we drove to the next town.

I say town. Really it was a tiny collection of old buildings in the desert. An old petrol garage. A few houses. Dry and dusty. I managed to get a mobile signal so I called the guys and told them where I was. It turned out that Stan and Harry had also been having difficulties: they had run out of fuel miles from civilisation while still in South Africa. They'd had to wait for a truck driver to pass and give them some spare diesel before continuing on their trek to fix the windscreen. Then they'd had trouble with their paperwork at the Namibian border. All these issues had caused a significant delay.

I found a tiny restaurant where I bought some food and a little more water. It would be an overstatement to call it a hotel, but they had a little room with a bed where I was able to catch some shuteye and wait for the guys to arrive.

The next day, we drove back to the point where the pick-up truck had collected me, and I carried on from there. My 24 hours alone in the desert had taken its toll, however. My body was tired and a strong headwind blew south. But I didn't want to rest. I wanted to carry on. It was tough to get going again, but as we had grown accustomed to saying: the game's the game.

And the game was about to get harder.

12

CHUNDERING GEEZER

Namibia is one of the most sparsely populated countries in the world. It spans an area of 824,000 square kilometres and shares its borders with South Africa to the south, Botswana to the east, Angola to the north and the Atlantic Ocean to the west. It's one of the most politically stable countries on the continent of Africa, with strong local communities and an economy driven by mining, agriculture, tourism and fishing. It was colonised by the Germans in the late nineteenth century, and gained independence from South Africa in 1990. As in South Africa, a noticeable proportion of the population was white. We met a good number of Afrikaner farmers as we headed north. Like their South African counterparts, they kept themselves separate from the Black population.

The geography of Namibia is varied. The Namib Desert – thought to be the oldest desert in the world – stretches along the coast. Inland, the terrain comprises rugged mountains in the central plateau and the broad savannah of the Kalahari Desert. My route would take us along the western fringes of the Kalahari. It's a hard, rocky landscape, unforgiving and relentless. We followed the B1 road – the country's principal national highway – for almost the entire length of the country. No left, no right. Day after day of ultramarathons on the same road, with up to a week between the infrequent towns.

As Jarred had to go on holiday, we needed a temporary replacement. A friend of a friend of Jarred's ran a tour-guide company in Namibia. He introduced us to Nessie, a Black Namibian man. Nessie was brilliant. He barely spoke any English, but he spent his time with us thinking carefully about how he could be of most use to the mission. I noticed that he went out of his way to help me as much as he could. Each time I took a break he would set out a chair for me, and a table with little plates of food. He would regularly cook for us. As we journeyed through the country, though, his presence taught us something about the culture. From time to time we would stay overnight in a comfortable lodge. These lodges tended to have segregated accommodation. The guests would stay in one part, the tour guides in another. As we were white and Nessie was Black, it was routinely assumed that he was our tour guide and he would be shown to the segregated accommodation. We would, of course, always correct that assumption and explain that Nessie was an integral part of our team. There was never a problem with this, but the assumption revealed the implicit hierarchies of race. Nobody was unkind or offensive to Nessie, but his treatment was, I suppose, a kind of racism and it reminded us of the privilege we commanded as white men in this part of the world.

We expected to encounter dangerous places on our mission but, in truth, despite the warning of the border guards, Namibia was not really one of them. That didn't mean, however, that our time in that country was without its challenges, and we were not naïve.

We always knew danger was on the cards. I would often run after dark. Nessie was not keen on this idea. He told us that it wasn't safe to be on the road after sunset, and he was soon proved right. The guys were waiting for me further along the road one evening when a car pulled over in front of them. Two guys got out of the front at the same time. They looked shifty. Nervous. Like they were up to no good. One of them grabbed something from the car. It looked suspiciously like a rifle or a shotgun. The guys hit the gas and sent me a message to say they were coming back to pick me up.

It was frustrating. I felt I still had more miles in my legs, but the incident made Nessie more adamant that I should not be out running after dark. The van seemed to be more of a target than me as an individual – nobody expected to see a lone runner by the side of the road carrying barely anything, whereas tourist vans and camping vehicles carrying valuable goods were more commonplace. We came to the conclusion, however, that these kinds of events were happening too often, and that it would be irresponsible for us to ignore the advice of the local man on our team. He was especially concerned about certain remote stretches of road where he knew there were insufficient police numbers, and from that point on we stopped running at night and continued with that policy for several months. And we were more on our guard. Sometimes we'd stop for the night in a lay-by and become aware of other cars performing suspicious drive-bys, scoping us out. That usually meant it was time to move further off the road or, if we were near a settlement, to find a hotel for the night.

We'd been in Namibia for about a week when Harry and I both woke up in the van feeling rough. This was Day 24, and it was not the usual marathon-induced stiffness kind of rough. Every part of my body ached. Then I started to shit. And vomit. And I couldn't stop doing either.

There's no good time or place to get food poisoning. But if there is, a hot van in the middle of the Namibian desert while performing back-to-back ultramarathons would not be it. I was in a wretched state. I had to remain horizontal for the entire morning. Every time I stood up, I thought I would pass out. At about two o'clock I decided to get out on the road. I wanted to run every day, without a day off. If I didn't rouse myself, today would be a write-off. I managed six kilometres. It completely finished me. I was totally dehydrated and couldn't hold down any food. It meant I lacked the energy to run even another metre. I carried on, but walking – forward movement at all costs – with the sun beating down on me, my body shrieking in toxic discomfort, stopping regularly to puke by the side of the road. By the 21-kilometre mark the sun had set. I'd managed a half marathon. My legs had started cramping for the first time in the entire mission. It would have to do for the day.

We decided to drive to the nearest town and find a hotel for the night. I was desperately hungry but still couldn't stomach any food. I had a night's sleep of sorts. In the morning we drove back to our start point, where I tried to eat some food and promptly threw up yet again. I couldn't squander another day, though, so I put one foot in front of the other and continued along the good old B1. I was out of it, lightheaded and aching, practically delirious. It was comfortably the worst running experience of my life. The guys tried several times to make me stop, worried that if I overdid things I'd put myself out of action for several days. Stan called for medical advice and kept close in the van. My memory of that day remains a blur. I know that I nearly passed out on several occasions. But I managed a marathon. In the final few kilometres I gradually began to think more clearly. When the 42 kilometres were in the bag and I finally stopped after sundown, I felt like I'd woken up from a dream, like the events of the day hadn't really happened. It had been the most intense day yet.

I tried to eat again the following morning. Threw it all up. Ran a marathon. It was brutal, but perhaps slightly less brutal than the day before. The sickness was passing. The illness, though, was far from over.

• • •

Publicity was not the purpose of the mission. It was a necessary by-product. We'd received a bit of publicity before the mission even started, including an article on the BBC website. Now, we needed people to know about what we were doing in order to fund the expedition. As we ran through Namibia it became clear that this was happening. Our social media numbers continued to grow. People who had heard of us joined me to run stretches of the road. I received a video message of support from Mo Farah, a real British icon and someone I massively admired. We also met up with a guy called Ewie, who liked what we were doing and reached out to us on Instagram, offering us comfortable accommodation near Windhoek, the capital city.

Windhoek is situated almost in the geographical centre of Namibia. It has a population of nearly half a million, and is the cultural and governmental hub of the country, Namibia being so sparsely populated. The city marked an important point on our route because it was here that we needed to get our passports stamped with visas that would allow us entry into the next three countries: Angola, the Democratic Republic of the Congo, and Congo. Ewie not only offered us a place to sleep, take a hot shower and wash our clothes, he also organised members of the city's running clubs to run with me. So Windhoek did not just end up being a place where we dealt with tedious administrative tasks. I ran to the airport to find 100 Namibian running enthusiasts waiting for me, and a police escort. Together we ran about ten kilometres through the town, the police blue-lighting us, cars honking in support, and my companions motivating us with African chants as we ran into the night. A crazy, memorable moment on the road.

We left Windhoek assuming we'd never see it again. We were very wrong about that. Circumstances would soon dictate that we'd have to return. In the meantime, I encountered an alarming development with my health.

I'd not long recuperated from my bout of food poisoning when I stopped by the side of the road to urinate. My piss came out red. Not pink. Deep red. I remember standing there, watching the stream and thinking: *That's pretty messed up*. Maybe it had something to do with the food poisoning; maybe it was a different issue. I discussed my symptoms with the guys, who were immediately worried. They thought I should consult a doctor right away. I tried not to overreact and told them I'd give it a few days. I reckoned it would probably sort itself out. The game's the game.

It didn't sort itself out. Every time I took a piss it was some shade of red, brown or deep orange. I knew that blood in the urine could be a sign of something serious, but I didn't hurt and I didn't feel dramatically worse in myself than I had done before the food poisoning. So I carried on with my daily marathons. I still thought the symptoms would pass. I thought wrong.

You know how it is when you have certain symptoms and access to the internet. You can't help researching them. Our internet research led us to worry that I might be suffering from a condition called rhabdomyolysis – rhabdo for short – which can be caused by muscle injury. If you have rhabdo, the muscle fibres die and release their contents into your bloodstream. Rhabdo can lead to kidney failure, and kidney failure can lead, quite quickly, to death. Didn't sound great. As the days passed and the blood in my urine didn't subside, I began to feel worse in myself. Everything was starting to ache a lot more. The marathons were getting harder. It felt like something might really be wrong. So after the fifth or sixth day of pissing blood, I agreed to talk to a doctor.

We consulted Google. The nearest doctor's surgery was in a town about an hour's drive away. It was a small town, and the doctor's surgery was a very basic place in a tiny building. The doctor himself was in his sixties and spoke reasonably good English. He took a urine sample and ran some tests. Fortunately, the rhabdo test came back negative, but he told me that I had protein in my piss. I knew this was sub-optimal. Protein in your piss is a good indicator that there's something wrong with your kidneys, but it can also be caused by extreme dehydration and high-intensity exercise. Having been running daily marathons while evacuating myself from both ends with food poisoning, I guessed I ticked both boxes. I'd been running on nothing so my body had started using itself as calories. I'd lost a good deal of muscle mass, and my kidneys had stopped filtering the blood properly.

I told the doctor I was attempting to run the full length of Africa. He thought I was crazy. Why would anyone try to do such a thing? His prescription was predictable enough. He told me I had to stop running for a few days to see if the symptoms cleared up.

I had no enthusiasm for this course of action. My hope was still to continue the mission without a single day off. I decided not to take the doctor's advice, but to modify it. Instead of taking a day off, I'd lower the intensity of my running. But I wouldn't stop.

The guys didn't think this was a good strategy. They thought I should follow doctor's orders. They also knew, however, that I wasn't likely to be influenced once I'd made my decision to continue. And my mantra was always that I couldn't allow pain to affect my decision-making. If I allowed myself to stop, or even reduce my mileage substantially, simply because I was in discomfort, I would never run the entire length of Africa. So I returned to the point on my route where I'd stopped running, and I restarted the mission.

I managed to run for about ten minutes. Felt dreadful. Had to stop.

It was clear that the symptoms weren't simply going to disappear. Maybe the time had come to listen to some advice after all. Maybe the time had come to take a day off.

I stopped for the rest of that day, and the day that followed. One of the people we'd met in Windhoek had offered us accommodation in lodges along the road, and we stayed in one of these. The rest did me good. We spent my day off touring a national park where we saw lions, giraffes, elephants and rhinos. There had not been much opportunity to witness the wildlife of southern Africa so far, which was probably not a bad thing. This was big cat country. Staying in a lodge one evening, we'd seen a big cat of some description approach, and I'd certainly been a little more on my guard as I ran the following day. I couldn't allow myself to be overly concerned about that particular threat – it was part of the cost of doing business – although I did try to rationalise my way out of the fear of big cats. Every time I saw a goat or a cow by the side of the road, I allowed myself to relax a little, because surely the Namibian farmers would not allow their livestock to roam freely if there was a chance that a big cat might take them.

A bigger threat was honey badgers. Cute name, but not a cute animal. In fact, they're one of the most aggressive animals in the world. They're tiny beasts but are well known for their tendency to attack anyone and anything, including lions. They have thick, loose skin, but you can't safely grab them if they attack, because they can spin around inside their skin and bite you. Best avoided, and I managed to, although the guys picked me up one night having seen them on the road I'd been running, so perhaps I had a close escape.

Snakes, on the other hand, were everywhere. Like Indiana Jones, I hate snakes, and the chance of being bitten by one was much greater than the chance of encountering a big cat or a honey badger. I would see snakes daily, basking by the side of the road, mostly very small ones in southern Africa, though I saw a good few big boys as we made our way north. I had no means of identifying them, or of knowing whether they were venomous or not. I just kept my distance.

I hated the prospect of having to take a day off – it had never been part of the plan – but at least we managed to squeeze in a memorable experience by seeing some of the wild animals of Africa in a safe environment. And after 48 hours of no running, the blood in my piss finally cleared up. I still felt a bit rough, but I couldn't allow feeling rough to be an impediment to the mission. Worse was surely to come. So the morning after my full day off, I hit the road again and continued north.

• • •

Big things are made of little things. A year is made up of days. A day is made up of hours. My strategy throughout the entire run was to break up the mammoth task into small, manageable pieces. If I meant to run 60 kilometres in a day, I wouldn't focus on that headline number. Even for me, 60 kilometres would feel like a big ask. Instead, I'd mentally break it down into three sessions of 20 kilometres each. Already it would feel more bite-sized. I'd focus on the first 20 kilometres that I needed to get under my feet before I had my first rest. Even then, I wouldn't look at my watch for the first 10 kilometres. There was a power to knowing you had double figures behind you and single figures ahead, that you were halfway to your first rest stop. With five kilometres left, I'd be able to tell myself that my first session was practically done, because five kilometres was almost nothing. In this way, with the day broken down into chunks that I could easily handle, the total distance felt less daunting.

And so, with the days broken down into these smaller, more manageable units, the miles continued to add up and the Angolan border approached.

13

GUNPOINT GEEZER

The two countries we'd traversed had not been without incident. We'd had some pretty shaky encounters. A number of people that we'd met along the way had warned us, however, that what we had experienced so far had been 'Africa-lite'. Our sense was that the 'real' Africa was still to come, and that the next two countries on our itinerary – Angola and the Democratic Republic of the Congo – would present very different challenges, both in terms of culture and security. We were particularly warned about the dangers of the DRC. The consensus was that it was no place for tourists. Almost all of the South Africans and Namibians we spoke to warned us off entering that country. The dangers of Angola were less dramatically stated, but there was undoubtedly a feeling that, when we crossed our next border, things would start to get a little more real.

As the border approached, we said goodbye to Nessie. Jarred was returning from holiday and so the time had come for our Namibian guide to leave us. He urged us to continue our policy of not running at night. There was, he said, a greater police presence in Angola than in Namibia, but the roads could still be dangerous. We listened hard to what he had to say. Nessie had been a force for good in the team and we were sorry to see him go. We had to keep

151

looking forwards, however, and that meant turning our attention to the next border crossing.

I had already begun to learn that border towns in this part of the world tended to be a little sketchy. A little livelier than other places. Perhaps it's because they are melting pots, places where travellers congregate as they overland the continent. Perhaps it's because they become a focus for any tensions that exist between countries. Whatever the reason, I think we all felt a little apprehensive on the day we were due to hit the border between Namibia and Angola. The guys in the van had heard gunshots earlier in the day. We never found out where the gunshots had come from, but they understandably put the guys on edge.

Inevitably, we experienced another problem with the van that day when a tyre burst two kilometres from the border. It delayed the guys, and meant that once more I reached the border alone. What a ballache. Locals posing as fixers crowded the crossing. As soon as I rocked up there, a crowd formed around me – pushy guys offering to change my money, to sort out all the documents I needed, to fill in this form, to speak to that official. They hustled hard and remained impervious to my attempts to lose them. It was stressful, and I was so obviously a target that a policewoman came to rescue me. She said I could wait for my friends in a little police building, out of the reach of most of the hustlers and the fixers. When the guys caught up with me, they had all our documents in order and we left Namibia without too much delay. One fixer who we hadn't managed to shake off took us through some winding corridors to a visa office, where we sat for two hours waiting for an official to have his lunch break. Finally, though, we dealt with all the red tape and were allowed to enter Angola.

The Angolan unit of currency is the kwanza. It has suffered from high inflation, and was undergoing another period of devaluation as we entered the country. There are no coins in usage, as their value has become so small as to render them worthless, and our Namibian dollars and South African rand were exchanged for huge bundles of notes. As soon as we agreed to change money with one guy, a whole crowd of others started hustling us, wanting a piece of the action. At one point, a mob surrounded the van, shaking it, putting their heads through the windows. It all started to kick off a bit, and I lost my head a little, shouting back at the hustlers until they all backed off.

Angola immediately seemed different. It was much busier than Namibia, much more populated and, to a Western eye, more stereotypically 'African'. At the border itself, the buildings were made of brick and concrete, but you didn't have to travel far for things to become more ramshackle. Motorbikes were much more common than cars, livestock was knocking around all over the place, and it was noisy: the sound of the bikes, the street hawkers, the general chaos of life in this crowded country was overwhelming. It was chaotic, but in a good way. If we felt uncomfortable, it was because our surroundings felt different to Namibia. There were very few white people to be seen, and we were experiencing the strangeness of the new. People shouted at me as I ran through the border town, but not in a threatening way. I met up with the guys at a petrol station on the edge of town. Two Angolan men stood guard, armed with AK-47 assault rifles. We certainly hadn't seen that in Namibia, but we soon realised that any shop in Angola that held items of value hosted armed guards. As we were obviously tourists, these guards evidently assumed that we were unlikely to be any trouble, so we didn't have any problems with them.

But we were wary. While we were in Angola somebody sent us a video of two criminals being punished by a mob in the capital city of Luanda. They were beaten to death in front of a cheering crowd, then set alight. Rumours reached us that police brutality in the Angolan police force was commonplace and that private security companies routinely took matters of law enforcement into their own hands, whether or not they had the right to do so. It would be lazy, though, to characterise that country through the prism of such rumours. Angola was a place of contradictions, and very obviously a product of its history.

The Portuguese first colonised Angola in the sixteenth century, enslaving locals and capitalising on resources such as rubber, oil and diamonds. The country declared its independence in 1975, but was soon plunged into a brutal civil war that lasted for more than 25 years. The Angolan civil war was primarily fought between two factions: a communist faction backed by the Soviet Union and Cuba, and an anti-communist faction backed by the USA and South Africa. The impact of that civil war on the people of Angola was devastating. Hundreds of thousands of people died. Millions were displaced. The conflict ended in 2002, but remnants and reminders of Angola's war-torn past remain. Unexploded landmines litter the countryside. The dilapidated shells of tanks and armoured vehicles lie discarded by the side of the roads. The Angolan civil war might have ended more than 20 years ago, but its scars are still visible.

So are the effects of the precarious economic situation the country has experienced in the intervening years. We often passed half-built, abandoned buildings – shopping centres, high schools and other infrastructure projects that had been started and then abandoned, presumably because the money had run out. The thing that people had told us about South Africa and Namibia being 'Africa-lite' came back to us; we could see what they meant. The standard of living was obviously lower here.

Our experience of the Angolan people, though, was that they exuded a sense of hope and unity. Many people told us that they were tired of the wars and strife that had blighted their country, and that life there was now more peaceful than it had been in years. They were friendly. We felt welcome, despite the language barrier we encountered. In South Africa and Namibia, English had been commonly spoken, alongside a variety of local dialects. The further we travelled from the Angolan border, the less common English became. Almost everybody spoke Portuguese, but that wasn't much good to us. Harry's Spanish was the closest we were able to get.

By this stage of the mission we had developed a 'roll with it' mentality. We knew that obstacles would continue to present themselves, but we couldn't worry about it too much. I probably adopted this mentality more than the others. I had to run 60 kilometres every day. I just had to put my head down and do it. It meant suppressing any nervousness I might have felt about the route, my health, difficulties on the road or the dangers that we might face in countries such as the DRC. It also meant separating myself to some extent from the anxieties of the team. I had my job to do, and I couldn't worry too much about them. That's not to say we were blasé. The risk of unexploded landmines and other improvised explosive devices (IEDs) was real. Angola is one of the most heavily mined countries in the world, with more than a thousand minefields and over a million unexploded devices. People had started to warn us about that particular danger back in Namibia. In Angola, the locals all offered the same advice: don't stray too far from the road. If you do leave the road to camp at night, stick to established tracks. To step on an IED wouldn't just bring an end to the mission, it might well bring an end to a life.

Despite these dangers, we settled comfortably into Angola. The countryside was beautiful and the people delightful. I noticed that the Angolans who joined me on the road tended to be more affluent, more middle class. It made sense: these were the type of people who would be interested in running as a pursuit, whereas the poorer Angolans were evidently baffled that anyone should do such a thing. As I ran through more rural regions, I became more acutely aware of my own privilege. As a younger man back in the UK, I would have thought of myself as working class. I might even have thought that I lacked opportunity. My experiences so far in Africa made me cringe to remember that mindset. In Angola I saw semi-naked children with malnourished pot bellies playing in stagnant lakes of water filled with shit and rubbish. The first time I encountered such a sight, I stopped running and watched, horrified.

I thought about going over to talk to them, to explain that this was not healthy or smart. I didn't, partly because I spoke no Portuguese and I knew that they would speak no English, partly because I was uncertain if it was my place to intervene. These experiences on the road, though, made me understand how lucky I had always been. I'd had the opportunity of an education. I had a flat and a car at 17. At 21 I'd been able to travel round the world. And although we were attempting this mission on a shoestring, the very fact that I had the opportunity to attempt it at all meant that my privilege was many times greater than that of the poorer Angolans whose villages and towns we passed through. Our sense of ourselves and our lives is a question of perspective, and there's no doubt that mine was changing.

Angola also taught me something about the importance of communities. I would run through little villages and, poor though they were, my sense was of tiny groups of people who supported each other in a way that never seemed to happen back in the UK. I didn't feel like I was running into a village, I felt like I was running into one massive family. For sure, the villagers took on traditional gender roles – the women would congregate to cook and look after the children, while the men would busy themselves with farming or other chores. And it would be trite of me to suggest that the sense of community in any way made up for the poverty of these rural Angolans. But as I ran through that country, I had time and motivation to reflect on my own life. I realised that the hardest times I'd experienced had been those when I'd felt alone, lacking guidance and separated from my family. Out here, in the Angolan countryside, the importance of those aspects of life crystallised in my mind.

It's impossible to run through Africa as a white man without your mind turning to the impact of colonisation. I was no historian. I didn't understand the impact of the past on the people I saw as I ran. All I knew was that many of the villages I saw lacked the basic infrastructure that we in the West take for granted. But we take something else for granted in the West: that we've got it all right. That our way of life is superior in every way to that of the impoverished on the continent of Africa. That we have all the answers. Now I was beginning to query this. No doubt these villagers lack much that we have, but we lack something they have: a sense of community that is diminishing in wealthier parts of the world. I started to question the idea that Africa has much to learn from us. Maybe it does, but maybe we have much to learn from Africa too.

I continued speaking to Emily for a couple of hours almost every day. I felt comfortable discussing whatever was on my mind, although I tried hard not to share with her anything that I thought would worry her. So I played down the occasional dangers of the road and avoided any mention of the warnings we'd received about entering the Democratic Republic of the Congo. Instead we talked about the logistics of the mission. We talked about my anxieties regarding the team and my ability to lead it. Often, we discussed these thoughts I was beginning to have about the importance of community. We spoke about family, and God. These were familiar concepts to Emily, and we talked about how I would like to introduce them into my own life. It wasn't lost on me that, although we were separated by many thousands of miles, our approaches to life were becoming more closely aligned. I felt like Emily had always understood what was important in life and that now, thanks to my mission, I was beginning to catch up.

My body felt good over the first couple of weeks in Angola. The ones and twos passed well and we made good time. I did some of the best running of the mission. Strong, fast marathons. On one day I averaged 5 minutes 32 seconds per kilometre, and I felt that I could maintain that consistency as long as circumstances went our way.

Unfortunately, they didn't.

The threat of malaria increased as we headed north. I would spray myself with insect repellent, especially at night, but that didn't offer full protection from mosquito bites. In Angola, I started taking a medication called Malarone. It's probably the most effective anti-malaria drug, but it has side effects. For me, the side effect was severe grumpiness. It affected my mood dramatically. Other matters compounded that grumpiness. On several occasions, the guys had been an hour or so late picking me up at the end of my run. They had their reasons, of course. They were busy with their own tasks, like editing, sourcing accommodation, finding food, buying petrol and carrying out all the logistical necessities that the mission required. It was difficult, with only one vehicle, to fit all that in around my requirements. When they were late, though, it drove me mad. Having broken my day into little units of 20 kilometres, and each unit of 20 kilometres into blocks of five, suddenly to have to run another five kilometres in failing light was a real drag. It brought me down. I spoke to the guys about it on several occasions, and I spoke to them about it again on the evening of Day 62. The guys took it well, and assured me that they'd be especially mindful of the pick-up times. I also made the decision to stop taking the malaria medication. I would just have to risk the chance of infection.

So the next morning, on the outskirts of the coastal town of Benguela, having worked out what it was that had affected my mood so profoundly, I felt pretty good. I felt strong. Instead of telling the guys to meet me after my first 20 kilometres, I told them to meet me after 30. I figured it would make the logistics easier for them if I required fewer pick-ups. It was an encouraging start to what I hoped would be an encouraging day.

When the time came for them to meet me for my first break, Stan stayed editing in the hotel where we were staying, while Jarred and Harry drove through an industrial district and parked the van a hundred metres from where I was running. It didn't feel like a dangerous area. Certainly it felt less dangerous than many we'd been through. There were people around, and vehicles. I reached the van having finished my first stint and sat in it with the guys, a bag of crisps in one hand and a mango juice in the other. It was early afternoon – maybe one or two o'clock. We were shooting the shit, nothing out of the ordinary, when suddenly the door of the van opened. Someone was standing there. My first thought was that a couple of locals wanted to say hello. Seemed a bit keen, but whatever.

Then I saw the gun.

Three guys had drawn up alongside us on a motorbike. Two had jumped off and opened the side door of the van. One of them erratically waved a pistol at us. Both were visibly pumped up. Panicked even. When we raised our hands, the guy with the gun jabbed it to indicate that we should lower them. Clearly they didn't want anybody to see what was going on. They shouted at us in Portuguese and although I didn't understand their words, I definitely understood their meaning: 'Give us everything you have!'

Harry managed a few words of his Spanish-Portuguese hybrid. '*Tranquillo*,' he said, trying to calm them down. '*Tranquillo, tranquillo*.' He pointed at a brown box under one of the seats. This was where we stowed everything of value, including our cash and our passports. They took its contents. They stepped foot into the van, half in half out, then they spotted one of our expensive cameras and a drone. They took these, too. Jarred had his phone out. They grabbed it, then demanded that the rest of us hand over our phones. Harry managed to fob them off with an old phone he used for music. I shook my head. 'Don't have a phone,' I said. I stood up to block their access to the rest of the van. Their demeanour was so aggressive, and they so clearly wanted the robbery to be over quickly without too much of a scene being made in public, that I felt almost certain they wouldn't risk firing their gun.

The guys, concerned for my safety, pushed me back into my seat, but as soon as the robbers encountered that moment of resistance, I could tell that they felt a little more uncertain of themselves. They didn't insist on me handing over a phone. They just backed off, carrying our camera gear and the contents of the brown box away from the van and onto their motorbike. Harry asked them to leave the passports. They ignored him. Then they buzzed off.

I was so angry. Obviously, nobody's life is worth risking for a passport or a phone, but part of me felt like we should have stood up to them more robustly. But what was done was done. We couldn't change the past, we just had to deal with the outcome. We went straight to the nearest police station and reported the crime. The police acted surprised that such a robbery had taken place, and I believed they were. We accompanied three of them back to the scene. Two wore uniforms and had their handguns on show. The third wore plain clothes and was pretty gangster. 'If we find them,' he said in Portuguese, 'they're done for.' I didn't know what that meant, but it sounded terminal and, again, I believed him. I didn't really think, though, that our assailants were in much danger. No doubt they were far away by now. Our stolen gear was probably already on its way to Zimbabwe. Nor did I feel particularly negative towards the robbers. I knew nothing about their situation or what had driven them to steal from us. I knew I could never put myself in their shoes. All my focus, really, was on the consequences of the robbery on the mission.

The robbers had stolen about six grand's worth of camera equipment. Not ideal, and if this had happened before we'd persuaded sponsors to come on board there's a good chance it would have spelled the end of the mission. However, as we now had a little money in the pot, we knew we could replace the gear. The loss of the passports, though, was a much bigger pain in the backside. We each had two passports – a main passport and a backup. The robbers hadn't taken our backups, but the problem was that my main pass-port, and Jarred's, contained all the visas we required for the next several countries on our route. The loss of the passport meant the loss of the visas. We couldn't continue past Angola without them.

The robbery made international news. Hardest Geezer being held up at gunpoint was too tempting a headline. I found myself being interviewed on TV and we realised that more and more people all over the world were following our mission. They say that all publicity is good publicity. Well, maybe. The president of Angola clearly didn't take that view. A British guy being robbed by armed Angolan men was not a good look for a country that was trying to expand its tourism industry. Surely it would put people off visiting and spending their money there. So it was decided, at the very highest level, that for the rest of our time in Angola I was to be afforded the benefit of a police escort.

All the major embassies and consulates were situated in Luanda, the capital. We hoped that we would be able to replace our visas there. A good idea in theory. In practice, we hit a brick wall. I ran the 540 kilometres to the capital over the next ten days accom-panied by my police escort, a truck with five or six police officers sticking close to my heel. The guys in the van, who were carrying everything that remained of value, did not have this restriction. I was the guy with the Instagram page, the lone runner who was the face of the mission. The van was a much higher-value target, but it was me that the Angolan president wanted to keep safe.

It was a bit jarring to have the police escort, but the police offi-cers themselves were good fun to be with. We had a laugh together, even though they spoke no English and I spoke no Portuguese. I was famous, in their eyes. They seemed more concerned with taking selfies along the way than with my safety, although I suppose their very presence was a good deterrent to any more wannabe robbers. We made a strange convoy as we headed north along the coast, occasionally joined by Angolan runners who wanted to join me for stretches of the road.

Luanda is a major port city on the Atlantic coast of Angola, home to more than 8 million and the main administrative centre of the country. We arrived there on Day 74 of the mission. The traffic is notoriously bad. It grew worse as our convoy held everything up. The local running club arranged a reception for us by the side of the highway, with local musicians and the presentation of a medal, then we ran along the beautiful waterfront lined with palm trees. Courtesy of some Angolan supporters, we were put up in a five-star hotel where we benefitted from the luxury of a comfortable bed and a hot shower. A good start to our stay in Luanda, but things were about to take a frustrating turn as we went about the business of replacing our visas.

Rather than the police escort, a private security company escorted us around town. Nobody, however, seemed set up to help out a British guy trying to run the length of Africa. This embassy had run out of stamps. That consulate only provided visas for Angolan citizens. They offered convoluted workarounds, but none of them worked for us because they would cost money we couldn't afford and – crucially – would mean skipping sections of the route. Not an option.

We wasted five days in the capital – five increasingly frustrating days without running – before we received a series of hard nos, and realised that we'd have zero success in Luanda. Jarred and I would have to travel to the nearest major city where we could be sure of acquiring visas. Trouble was, the nearest such city was Windhoek.

Back in Namibia.

Two thousand kilometres away.

Result.

The last thing we wanted was the hindrance of a police escort all the way back to the Namibian border. We decided not to tell them that we were obliged to make this tedious detour. We climbed back into the van and floored it south. We didn't stop. We took turns sleeping and driving. We re-crossed the border into Namibia and sped south back along the familiar route of the B1 to Windhoek. We spent several days back in the Namibian capital sourcing new visas. Back at the Angolan border, we realised our Angolan visas had expired and so we were delayed further while an expensive 'emergency' visa was sourced. By the time we returned to Luanda, we'd lost about two weeks and several thousand pounds. I was desperate to get my feet back on the tarmac.

I realise now, looking back, that the Angolan incident caused a shift in my thinking. Our reaction to being held up at gunpoint had been entirely understandable, entirely human. Scared for our lives, we'd done exactly what most people would have done and handed over the objects that were of most value to us. We'd given the robbers what they'd wanted in order to bring the incident to an end. Almost anybody else in our place would have done the same. To expect my team to act in any other way would have been to pile an unreasonable amount of pressure on them and I couldn't do that. They'd followed to the letter the standard advice for such situations. De-escalate. Put your own safety first. Even then, the long-term effects of the incident had been bad. In the days and weeks that followed, I noticed a general sense of anxiety among the guys, which I completely understood on a human level. Who wouldn't feel anxious after such an event?

But there was a flip side. The harsh reality of our mission was that results mattered. In giving the robbers our passports, we'd been thrown badly off course. I found myself wondering if there existed potential teammates who *could* cope with having placed upon them what others would consider an unreasonable amount of pressure. Did potential teammates exist who had experience of terrifying situations like the one we'd just encountered, and who knew how to deal with them safely but also without compromising the mission? I didn't know the answer to these questions. I certainly didn't raise the subject with the guys. I didn't blame them for the circumstances in which we found ourselves. If anything, I blamed myself for my inadequacies as an expedition leader. I knew from experience that I couldn't make changes in the team and for there to be a nice, amicable outcome. I lacked the communication skills, and in any case the guys had already committed so much to the mission. We'd been through a lot together. But the thought was there, and it wouldn't go away.

We reconnected with our police escort in Luanda and, after that long and frustrating hiatus, hit the road again on Day 89.

From a personal point of view, I wouldn't have chosen to have that escort. I didn't massively relish the attention it attracted, and there were moments when the jurisdiction of one police force finished and the jurisdiction of another started. This meant the officers had to change shifts and I was forced to wait for a few hours when I'd rather have been tearing up the tarmac. It had its advantages, though. It was good for our content and raised awareness of the mission, and it meant that our remaining time in Angola ran smoothly. There was certainly something reassuring about having an armed police presence as I ran through some of the sketchier slums on the outskirts of Luanda.

But there was one further unwelcome side effect of our escort: the police didn't want to stay overnight by the side of the road. On occasion they let us stay in police stations, but mostly they insisted that we check into hotels. Those hotels gave us another insight into the difference between Angola and the two countries we'd passed through so far. They were much more humble places, with few facilities, dodgy sanitation and buckets of water instead of showers. These hotels – like everything in Angola – were expensive. Inflation had done its work and the economy was not thriving. It was an outlay we could have done without.

There were other problems. The two-week hiatus we'd endured had not only been frustrating, it also had a noticeable effect on my body. I managed to put on a bit more bulk but, having run ultramarathons almost every day for 74 days, my body clearly thought I'd stopped doing this weird thing to it. It had relaxed into its new, easier way of life. When I restarted running, the tightness and inflammation returned. My hamstrings, quads and knees were in pain. I found myself having to reacclimatise to the relentless nature of the mission and there were moments when I couldn't run for more than 10 or 15 minutes at a time. But the brutal truth was that I couldn't ease myself in slowly. The two-week hiatus had been wasted time. I only had 3,700 kilometres behind me. I still had more than 11,000 kilometres to run, and that number wasn't going to get any smaller if I wasn't out on the road, putting in the distance. Those were tough runs. I limped badly and the pain when walking was far greater than any pain I'd experienced when running before the hiatus. My fitness levels required me to take more frequent breaks, but I didn't stop putting in the marathons. I knew I had to go through this pain barrier to get my body re-accustomed to the process. It was just a question of beating my legs into the tarmac, hour after hour, day after day.

Gradually, the pain, stiffness and inflammation eased off. The temperature and humidity, however, increased as we moved north. The heat made it hard to sleep at night. The terrain changed too. It became greener. More jungly. Like something out of *Jurassic Park*. I felt ready for a T-Rex to jump out of the bushes at any moment. And I knew what this change of terrain meant: one of the biggest challenges of our mission was approaching. Within days, we would be at the border of one of the most dangerous countries in the world: the Democratic Republic of the Congo.

14

JUNGLE
GEEZER

We'd seen plenty of impoverished, run-down villages in Angola, but my sense was that the government took pride in its official buildings. This extended to the control posts at the border with the DRC, where brick-built buildings gave the impression at least of officialdom and infrastructure. The buildings on the DRC side of the border, however, were completely different. Little more than shacks, and without question the least developed conditions we'd seen so far in Africa. We were required to undergo a medical check on entry. This took place in an old tent, but there was no real medical check to speak of. Just a form to fill in and an outstretched palm from an official, demanding money. 'What for?' I asked.

'Because you give me a present,' he said, his eyes steely.

I shook my head. We'd grown accustomed to officials asking for bribes, and bolder when it came to rejecting them.

We changed some currency and bought SIM cards, not from an official shop – there was no such thing – but from a guy selling them on a carpet among stalls hawking fruit and other bits and bobs. We negotiated our way through the bustle and past a final barrier where another official wanted us to pay a road tax. We had to insist that our little four-berth van was not the 20- to 30-seater he claimed it was, which would attract a much higher fee. It took two hours of negotiating to bring the tax down from £95 to £20, during which time village kids surrounded the van, banging on it, shaking it, looking through the windows, asking for money. If we opened the door at all, they'd reach inside and try to grab stuff. They even managed to take a few things before sprinting away.

There was no doubt about it: the moment we set foot on DRC soil, the intensity level shot up.

When we'd crossed from Namibia to Angola, we'd immediately noticed a change in our environment. Crowded towns, poorer infrastructure, increased poverty. Crossing into the DRC represented another shift. The first town we hit, Matadi, was properly chaotic, probably one of the busiest places we'd seen. The roads were poor, just a mishmash of dirt, gravel and sand. Any shops we saw were little wooden shanties selling a meagre collection of goods. At a petrol station we encountered several heavily armed guards. We'd seen this in Angola, of course, but these guys seemed like a much more serious proposition. Fuel was as expensive in the DRC as in the UK. Armed gangs frequently attacked petrol stations to steal it. There was traffic everywhere, but no road markings or any sense of there being a highway code. It was every man or woman for themselves. As in Angola, hundreds of motorbikes buzzed around, and there was a huge range of cars, from clapped-out, beaten-up old wrecks to hugely luxurious Mercedes. The distinction between these two types of vehicle was in your face, and immediately told us something about the gulf between the haves and the have-nots in the DRC. We stayed that night in a hotel. It was expensive, far out of the reach of your average citizen, frequented only by government officials or businesspeople. But your money didn't buy you much. The shower didn't work. The door didn't lock.

The citizens of Angola, in general, had always seemed pleased to see us. Sure, we'd had our moment with the armed robbery, but for the main part they appeared friendly and welcoming. And while it would be wrong of me to generalise, we immediately sensed that this was not the case in the DRC. Menace hung in the air. Hostility. In the preceding countries, when people had tried to extort money from us, there had been a little lubing up beforehand as they at least tried to make us feel good about the transaction. There had always been a twinkle in the eye. Not here. An assumption existed – here more than anywhere else – that as white tourists we had money, and were therefore a target. A language barrier remained, which didn't help. The citizens of the DRC spoke French, Lingala and a variety of other dialects. Harry spoke a little French. I could manage '*Bonjour*' and an occasional '*Ça va?*' If I needed to talk my way out of a difficult situation, it would be a problem.

I didn't enjoy my first full day of running. My experience so far had been that, while people in rural areas tended to be friendlier than those in the cities, the bustle of the cities made me feel quite safe. With so many people around, the risk of a dodgy encounter was lower. Here, in the DRC, I did not have that feeling. There was no comfort in a crowd. As I ran through Matadi, I attracted much unwelcome attention. People followed me closely – worryingly closely – on motorbikes. They tried to urge me – lure me – into their houses, such as they were. Passers-by shouted aggressively at me. I couldn't understand the language, but I knew this: they were not shouting 'Welcome to our country'. I felt like something bad could happen at any moment. I felt scared.

I did the only thing I could do: I kept running.

The Congo River is the second longest in Africa, after the Nile. It stretches from the Atlantic Ocean and through the capital city of Kinshasa before winding its way through the rest of this vast country. My first job, on leaving the city, was to cross the Matadi Bridge, one of the very few bridges that spans this enormous river. It's an impressive construction, a suspension bridge that for many years was the longest on the African continent. Busy, too, with more people on foot than in cars. The river flowed fast beneath me, and as I crossed the bridge I looked out over the intensely green terrain that awaited me. It was beautiful. Breathtaking, really. But I could have had no premonition of the dangers that awaited me in the interior of the DRC.

• • •

By any measure, the Democratic Republic of the Congo – formerly Zaire – is a troubled place. A series of brutal conflicts and human-itarian crises marks its recent history. The dictatorial rule of President Mobutu in the latter half of the twentieth century was characterised by corruption, nepotism and authoritarianism. He was overthrown during the First Congo War of 1996–7, which had been triggered by an influx of refugees and armed groups in the aftermath of the Rwandan genocide. The Second Congo War, which started the following year – also known as the Great African War – resulted in millions of deaths from fighting, disease and starvation. It was one of the deadliest conflicts since the Second World War. Even after it officially ended in 2003, armed groups continued to operate across the country, leading to the displacement of millions, food insecurity, malnutrition and outbreaks of diseases like Ebola and cholera. The country is rich in natural resources, which attract the attention of corrupt groups and lead to many abuses of human rights, including child labour. It is famously one of the most challenging environments in the world, and one of the least safe for visitors.

All in all, not the perfect place for a quiet jog.

On my second day in the DRC, I ran through a number of small settlements. The sense of hostility did not ease off in these more rural regions. As in Matadi, people would shout out at me, crowd round me and grab me as I ran. There was no chance of adopting the crazy geezer persona, as I did in South Africa. There, and in both Namibia and Angola, any aggressive locals I'd met had been limited to a few rogue individuals. Here, I felt threatened everywhere I looked. Practically everyone I passed shouted at me. I lost count of the number of people who tried to interfere. I knew the crazy geezer act would have just antagonised the locals. If it had kicked off, it would have been me versus a mob.

So I just kept my head down. I kept running.

I was passing through one of these villages, talking to Emily on my phone, when a guy pulled up to me on his motorbike – a beaten-up old thing with a tiny but noisy engine. He drove along-side me and shouted, '*Arrêtez-vous!*' *Stop!*

I shook my head. 'Nah, mate.' I carried on running.

He didn't give up. He continued alongside me. *Stop!*

I told Emily I had to go. We hung up. I carried on running.

Stop! By the third time of asking I could hear the aggression in his voice.

I didn't stop. Within a couple of minutes, however, three more motorbikes carrying six or seven guys in total had joined him. They stuck close. They shouted at me. I didn't stop. My only defence was to keep moving. But then, up ahead, I saw a fork in the road. I didn't know whether I had to run left or right. It meant stopping, getting out my big old expensive iPhone and checking the map. I never really liked getting my phone out in public. I didn't even like having my Garmin watch on display, and would cover it with my sleeve as I ran. To do anything else in poor areas felt ostentatious, and it felt like I was asking to be robbed.

Now, though, I had no option.

I stopped to take out my phone. The guys completely surrounded me. They barked at me, maybe in French, maybe in Lingala, I'm not too sure. I could tell they were angry but I didn't know what they were saying. All I knew was that there were too many of them for me to do anything about it. Even if I could get away, I couldn't outrun them when they were on motorbikes. They kept shouting at me until finally someone joined them who spoke some English. 'We need to check your passport,' he said.

Apparently, these hostile guys on motorbikes were some kind of government officials wanting to check my documents and visa.

Nothing about their clothing or demeanour indicated this. They wore no official uniform, just the same rough old ragtag clothes as everybody else. I didn't have my passport with me, so I had to call the guys and tell them join us. Once the men on motorbikes had seen our documents, they became less hostile and explained that they'd needed to check that we weren't terrorists. They explained that a white man on foot was an uncommon sight in this area. A suspicious sight. This was dangerous territory, they said. We needed to take care. They buzzed off, but I was left with post-adrenaline exhaustion and an uncomfortable sense of what might have happened had I been unable to show those men my passport.

The encounter unsettled me. I felt that I'd got to grips with the culture in the previous three countries through which I'd run. I felt like I was acclimatising to the strangeness of Africa. No longer. Here, officials chased you down on motorbikes. Locals heckled you for no reason. Everybody was aggressive. There was rubbish all over the place and poverty wherever you looked. This different world disorientated me completely.

That night, however, we saw a different side of life in the DRC when we stayed in a village. The guys had driven on ahead to ask permission of the village chief. Permission was granted, on the proviso that we made a small donation. One of the children in the village had something terribly wrong with his leg. He urgently needed medicine, but there was no money to pay for it. Hence the donation. It was one of the most basic settlements you could imagine. Villagers cooking on outdoor fires with cast-iron pots. Kids played in the dirt. Chickens and livestock wandered freely. The children of the village were excited to see us, especially when we showed them all our fancy camera equipment. The chief himself welcomed us warmly. We were to learn that village chiefs were generally one of the elders of the village and almost always a man – we only met one female village chief in all our time in Africa. Villagers would have maximum respect for the chief and he, along with any man of significant status in the community, would generally have three or four wives and many children.

As we were setting up camp, a man arrived in the village. He clearly suffered from some kind of disease. Open sores covered his skin, which had deteriorated in places to reveal raw flesh. He carried a heavy lump of rock from which ugly metal spikes protruded, and he brandished this rock as a weapon as he approached us. He demanded, in French, the equivalent of three pounds to get a taxi to the next village.

'Why?' I asked, and Harry translated.

'Because you're a white man,' he told me. 'You owe me this money because of what you have done in this country.' His tone was super-aggressive. So was his body language. He held up his vicious-looking weapon and I sensed that he meant to use it. We didn't want to give him any money. We knew that as soon as word spread that the tourists in the village would hand out money if you threatened them, we'd be inundated. At the same time, we didn't want to wind this guy up. We decided to give him the equivalent of one pound. The offer satisfied him and he went on his way, but the incident only consolidated our unease. Even here, in a friendly village with the approval of the chief, we were under threat. Nobody would feel an obligation to protect us.

I woke early on Day 102. Overnight I had decided that I wanted to put in a 100-kilometre shift that day. I'd made a commitment when we'd reached 100,000 subscribers to do a 100k day, but that wasn't the only reason. I wanted to get us out of the DRC as quickly as possible. The boys had planned a route with that aim in mind, heading north towards the Republic of the Congo. The tarmacked road would take us to the village of Kinkunda, and then cross country. It was still dark when I started running, and I felt the cloak of anxiety from the very moment I hit the road. As if something bad was around the corner. I completed my first 20 kilometres under an overcast sky, met up with the boys and ate some bread, which was about the only food we could find to eat in the DRC, with Nutella that we'd bought back in Angola. Then, after my rest and refuel, I started running again.

I turned, as planned, off the main road and onto a dirt track. I could see the van 500 metres up ahead. I ran up alongside it. The guys told me that they weren't sure if the road ahead was passable for the van, but some locals had told them there was another way round. We looked at the map and identified a place to meet in a couple of hours. The guys went to find their alternative route. I carried on running.

I found myself in true jungle terrain. Beneath my feet was just a dirt trail with motorbike tracks on it. The vegetation on either side was several metres high. I could see the sky – the sun had broken through the clouds and it was very hot and humid – but everywhere else I looked was thick, green, overgrown bush. The noise of the jungle surrounded me: the constant buzz and hum of insects, the occasional squawk or cry or slither of unseen birds or beasts. I'd pass the occasional human carrying a bucket of water or sitting on a motorbike and warily watching me pass, but this was not a heavily populated area. This was deep jungle. I had no mobile service.

I'd been running for an hour and a half when I heard the buzz of a motorbike behind me. I looked over my shoulder to see a solitary biker following me. He approached, drew up alongside me and tried to get me to stop. My experience with the officials the previous day hadn't made me any keener to engage with guys on motorbikes so I continued the ones and twos and tried to ignore him. He persisted. He was trying to show me something, so, after about 15 minutes, I stopped. The guy handed me a handwritten note, then disappeared.

The note was from the guys. The road to the meeting place had been impassable after all. They told me to meet them in the nearby village of Vanga.

The maps weren't properly loading on my phone. All I had was a vague sense of my trajectory, and that my path would take me along tiny single tracks and through two separate settlements before I reached the new meeting point. Distance? Fifteen or 20 kilometres, and I'd run out of water. I'm not going to lie: it felt in my head like things were getting a bit tasty. I made my away along footpaths that barely existed. I had to whack vegetation away to get through, and try not to think too hard about what might be lurking in that dense foliage. Snakes? Worse? I didn't want to know. I stumbled across the first little settlement, no more than a few huts, which I ran through as quickly as I could with my head down. The anxiety that had been with me since I'd woken was bubbling in my gut. I didn't want to speak to anyone. I wanted no interaction. I just wanted to find the guys. I passed that settlement without incident. Relief. Maybe everything would be all right.

I carried on, along a maze of little single tracks, each indistinguishable from the other. I lost my bearings. I didn't know which way I was heading. From time to time the foliage would become too thick and impassable, so I'd turn back on myself and wade across fast-moving streams in the hope of finding another path. This was supposed to be a 20-kilometre stint but I could tell from my watch that I'd racked up at least another five or six kilometres with my constant meandering detours.

Eventually, though, the second settlement came into view. I could see from a distance that it was a little more populated than the first, but I planned to follow the same strategy: to put my head down and run through it as quickly as possible.

Wasn't going to happen.

People started shouting at me as I attempted to cross the village. I ignored them. Kept on running. Villagers started chasing me and soon I was surrounded. There was no way through.

The chief of the village approached. He angrily started talking at me in Lingala. I couldn't understand a word he said, but I guessed he was furious with me for ignoring his guys and running through the village without his permission. I could also tell, from his gestures, that he wanted money.

I had none. I tried to communicate this. I also tried to communicate that I was sorry, that I was just passing through. He either didn't understand or didn't care. He grabbed me. Manhandled me. Pushed me around. By now, half the village had congregated to watch. About 50 people completely surrounded me, watching the argument as it unfolded with serious, hostile expressions.

The chief made an announcement. As one, all the women and children left the vicinity.

It didn't feel like a good sign.

I tried again to make myself understood and pointed in the direction I wanted to go. He shook his head. He pointed in a completely different direction. Then he selected two of his guys. They both carried large, curved machetes, commonplace in that part of the world because they are used as a tool to cut through the jungle foliage, but still not a reassuring sight for a lone stranger in a hostile situation. I understood that the chief was telling his guys to take me in the direction he'd selected. The wrong direction. Deep into the jungle.

I couldn't argue. The route I wanted to take was barred. My only option was to go with the men.

And my only thought was this: either they're going to rob me, and this is an act of intimidation to weaken my resistance, or they're going to kill me.

These were not exaggerated thoughts. We'd heard terrible stories about the Democratic Republic of the Congo. We had heard stories about tourists being killed for the watch on their wrist. So as we walked, I tried to communicate with the men.

I craved reassurance that I wasn't about to die, so I tried to be matey with them, and apologetic that I had no money, in the hope that I'd receive some hint of friendliness in return. They offered none. They just led me silently down a narrow, overgrown path, through a patch of thick jungle and into a little clearing. The path continued beyond the clearing, into the jungle. But here we stopped.

They said nothing. They simply clutched their machetes and stared at me.

I turned up the friendliness dial. I removed my rucksack. Opened it up. Found a packet of crumbled biscuits. Handed it to one of them. He looked at the biscuits. He looked at me.

And then I ran.

I didn't know what other option I had. I didn't run back to the village, of course. I took the path that led away from the clearing. They shouted at me. Tried to call me back. But they didn't chase. Or if they did I was too far away to see them.

Sketched out beyond belief, I sprinted and hacked my way through these jungle paths, my heart thumping, unaware of my location or direction, just desperate to put some distance between me and the machete men. To this day I don't know what the chief had told them to do or what they intended. As I ran, I heard noises all around me. The noises of the jungle, of course, but also the roar of motorbike engines, sometimes close, sometimes far away, their direction indistinct as they seemed to circle all around. I could hear groups of men shouting and laughing, their voices drifting above the jungle canopy. I could hear the sound of machetes slicing through vegetation. If a sound came too close, I'd jump behind a tree in utter panic and hide. Then I'd sprint again. Then I'd hide again. And in this way I stumbled through the bush with adrenaline burning through me.

Finally, I hit a road. A dirt road, for sure, but bigger and wider than the overgrown trails I'd been navigating. So far as I could tell, from my confused sense of the geography, it was the road to Vanga, the meeting point. I ran a couple more kilometres up the road until I came to the edge of the village. It looked a little more built-up than the previous two villages, although still not much more than a collection of mud huts. For obvious reasons, I was wary of entering Vanga by myself. I peered down the main road from the outskirts, looking for the van. It was pretty distinctive, so I reckoned that if the guys were there I would have seen it immediately.

I didn't see it. The van was nowhere in sight. The boys weren't there.

I'd covered approximately 50 kilometres that day. I'd run out of water and food. My phone was about to die and I had no signal anyway. Less than three hours of sunlight remained. I was alone, and fearful that the machete-wielding guys were searching for me.

And things were about to get worse.

15

HOSTAGE GEEZER

T his was my thinking.

    The last piece of tarmacked road I'd seen had been the main N1 road up to Kinkunda. This was the last stretch where I knew the boys could definitely drive the van. That was where they'd most likely returned for a rendezvous. If I didn't find them there, I could make my way back to the village where the chief had allowed us to camp the previous night. The last relatively friendly place I knew.

    I couldn't run – I was dehydrated and exhausted – so I chose to walk. The road was busier than the jungle paths I'd been following, but that didn't make me any less sketched out. I still worried that the machete guys were after me and, even if they weren't, my time in the DRC had taught me to be wary of the motorbikes that buzzed past me either way along the road. When, a few kilometres along the road, two guys on a motorbike pulled up alongside me and made gestures to indicate that I should go with them, you'll understand that I wasn't crazy about the idea. I shook my head. 'No,' I said, and I carried on walking.

    They were insistent. Their spoken language and their body language both said: you *have* to come with us.

    'Why?' I said.

And then they said, in French. '*Vos amis.*'

Amis? I recognised that word. It meant 'friends'.

I tried to weigh up the options in my head. It seemed to me that there were two possibilities. Either it was the case that Stan, Harry and Jarred had sent these guys to find me. Or, word had made it round the bush telegraph that a lone white guy was wandering around, and he'd make a good target for a robbing. The second possibility made me cautious. But by now I only had two hours of daylight left, and I still had no water, and I still had no mobile service. I hesitated. The guys were insistent. Twenty minutes we argued. Half an hour. I thought to myself, if they really *are* taking me to my friends, I'm safe. If they *aren't*, and they have some other plans for me, I'll know about it within 30 minutes and I can worry about it then.

I decided to get on the bike.

I expected them to head south. That was the direction in which I was most likely to find the van. That was the direction of the nearest tarmacked road. If they headed south, I was good.

They headed north.

Okay. Stay calm. Maybe they know some better route. Some shortcut. Maybe everything is all right.

As we passed through several villages, however, I sensed that they were taking me in exactly the wrong direction. Half an hour passed. I got off the bike. Shook my head. Stepped back. In broken English they insisted that I get back on. Their demeanour had changed. They hadn't been friendly beforehand, but now they were becoming more impatient. More hostile. Even more unwilling to take no for an answer. I tried to rationalise my situation. Maybe the boys had got stuck somewhere and this was the only route we could take to find them. So I climbed back on the bike, and we continued our journey.

By now I've been on the bike for an hour. I don't know what to do. I start testing them. Challenging them. Where are we going? What are we doing? The more I ask, the more aggressive they become.

And they don't stop.

I'm the third man on the back of a bike built for one. There's nowhere to rest my feet. I'm cramped and tense and holding on for dear life. I'm a massive, knotted ball of anxiety. The sun sets. Now it's night-time. The only source of light is the weak headlamp on the motorbike. It illuminates a narrow dirt track ahead, but not the dense jungle all around, thick with the screaming and the screeching of the forest at nightfall.

After an hour and a half, I have to accept that I've been kidnapped.

I think about jumping off the bike and running. But what then? Best-case scenario, I find another village. But my captors are going to keep looking for me. They have a bike; I'd be on foot. They'd know everyone; I'd know nobody. They'd soon find me. Worst-case scenario, I'm lost in the jungle at night, dodging whatever animals are out hunting, and the machete men, and the motorbike guys.

No. Jumping off isn't an option. I can't see where that plan takes me.

The men are talking. It's hard to understand them. I think they mention money. I think they mention the chief.

Not good.

Maybe I *should* run.

But I am weak with dehydration and hunger. I've covered more than a marathon today. Even if I wanted to run, I'm not sure I have the energy to do it.

I don't even have the energy to talk.

Or the courage.

Because as the hours pass, and the night becomes darker and the jungle thicker and the road rougher, and as the voices of my captors become harsher and more aggressive, and the feeling of horror grows in my gut, and the strength drains from my limbs, a dreadful conclusion settles on me.

I think to myself that if they were going to rob me, they'd have robbed me. So they must intend something else. I wonder if they might be taking me deep in the forest in order to put out a ransom. I have a few hundred thousand followers on Instagram, so perhaps they've wrongly calculated that I'm a person of wealth and influence. It doesn't seem likely. Far more likely is the possibility that they are taking me away from civilisation because they don't want anybody in the vicinity when they do to me what they mean to do. They want to take me somewhere my body will never be found.

I truly think I'm going die.

· · ·

They say that in the moments before your death, your life flashes before your eyes.

As I gripped the body of that juddering motorbike, I couldn't help but think how stupid I had been. I couldn't help but think that I had let everybody down. I'd left England without properly fixing things with my mum and dad. I imagined them receiving the news that I'd gone missing. I thought of the intolerable worry and stress. I pictured them at home, hearing that my body had been found. I wished I could speak to them, just once. I wished I could tell them that I regretted the way I'd handled things when I was younger.

I wished I could tell them that I was sorry.

I wished I could tell them that I loved them.

I'd always meant to. I'd always thought that, at some point, I'd reach out to my family and make amends for my mistakes. Now that chance had gone. They'd never know.

Since the age of 15 or 16, I'd largely done things by myself. In the last few months, though, since meeting Emily, I'd started to see a future where I could be happy with a family of my own. With her. I'd seen, running through Africa, the importance of family and community. I'd envisaged a version of my life that prioritised those values. I'd planned for it, during the long, lonely hours on the road.

And now I'd thrown it away.

I'd never believed, when I was younger, that my life would amount to much. Even at the start of the Africa mission, when I was skint and the project looked uncertain, it felt unlikely that my future held such conventional pleasures as a nice house and a happy family. As the mission had progressed, though, I'd begun to wonder if such a version of my life existed. The carrot had been dangled. And now, through my carelessness, the carrot had been ripped away.

I cried on the back of that motorbike, as two hours became three and three hours became four. I cried for my family. I cried for Emily. I cried for myself.

I didn't pray. Not in the conventional sense. Emily and I had discussed God, and I was on my way to thinking of myself as a Christian. But who was I to ask God to intervene? Four hours became five and five became six. I was still on the back of that bike, still lost, still scared, still filled with bitter regrets, so I started a conversation in my mind with God. If He was out there, He knew what was best for me. He knew that all this was part of a wider plan. I just had to accept that whatever was happening to me now was meant to happen for a reason I didn't understand. I felt a kind of peace descend.

Maybe I would live.

Maybe I would die.

I couldn't fight the uncertainty. I couldn't write the end of this story. It was out of my hands.

I remained on that bike for seven hours. The longest, hardest seven hours of my life.

• • •

We arrived in the middle of the night at a village called Sumbi.

Sumbi sat on a junction with a main road, the N12. There weren't many cars on that road. Just the occasional four-by-four. People were out on the streets even though it was night-time. I felt all eyes on me as my captors led me to a building by the roadside. A wooden shack with a tin roof. Confused, terrified and under duress,

I stumbled into that building. There was an old table inside and a few chairs. Six men were waiting for me. They emanated hostility. My captors gave me a chair and indicated that I should sit. I did as I was told and sat quietly as the men started to argue. I didn't know for sure what was the subject of their argument, but I figured it was me. Another nine or ten men arrived over the next 45 minutes, and the argument grew more aggressive. The men shouted at each other. They pointed in my direction. Then they shouted some more.

I stayed quiet. I didn't move. These events were out of my control. I tried to work out the social hierarchy. The motorbike guys, it seemed to me, occupied one of the lower rungs. They were not important men. People were bossing them around. Then another man arrived. He clearly had some authority; the body language of the others told me that he commanded respect. He was the chief.

The chief approached. He stood over me. He stared.

Then he said: 'You speak to me in English, very slowly.'

A wave of relief washed over me. It wasn't just that I'd found someone I could communicate with, it was that he *wanted* to communicate. Perhaps I wasn't going to die after all.

'There's been a big mistake,' I said. 'I'm sorry. I wasn't meant to be here ... '

'What are you doing in the Congo?' the chief interrupted me.

His question reassured me. He wouldn't be asking me that if the decision had been made to do something terrible.

'I need to speak to my friends,' I said. 'I have a number. Can we call them?'

The chief considered that request for a moment. Then he nodded.

A bunch of the men led me to another building. They called it the police station, but really it was just another shack. I gave them Harry's WhatsApp number. They called the number and spoke to Harry in French, telling him that they needed to come and get me, and that they needed to bring money.

. . .

You can imagine the guys' relief when they received that call. I'd been missing for many hours, and they too had experienced difficult times.

After I'd left them the previous morning, they'd tried and failed to drive the van along their intended route. They'd sent the first motorbike guy to give me the message to meet them in Vanga, but they couldn't get there because that road was also impassable by van. So they returned to the village where we'd stayed the night and offered the friendly chief a bunch of money to send some motorbikes out to find and transport me to the village of Sumbi.

We think the chief paid another trusted guy to supply the motorbikes, while taking his own cut of the transaction. The trusted guy turned out not to be quite so trustworthy and simply offered money to a whole array of people to find me and transport me to Sumbi. In this way word spread that a lone white guy was running through the jungle. Anyone who found him and delivered him to Sumbi could expect a pay day. My two captors thought they'd be paid, but so did many other motorcyclists cruising through the jungle. There was a bounty on my head, I just didn't know it. And I wasn't leaving Sumbi until money passed somebody's palm.

It meant the guys had to come and get me. I asked the chief of the village if one of his guys could take me to them. That way I could be on the road quicker. No way. They had to come to me with the money. I was not allowed to leave Sumbi until debts were settled. I was, in effect, a hostage in that village.

They gave me a room with a piece of foam on a wooden base. I wasn't the only inhabitant of that room. I could hear rats scurrying around, chewing at the wood. Not that it mattered. It was a relief just to lie down and know that I was relatively safe, for now. I closed my eyes and reflected on the carnage of the day. I reflected on the fact that I felt lucky to be alive. And, for a few hours, I slept.

The chief woke me early. I was in a pretty bad way. I hadn't drunk for 24 hours, during which time I'd run more than a marathon in jungle heat and humidity. I was given some rice and beans. More importantly, I was given some water. Then I was presented to a village elder – the guy who I thought was the chief was clearly his number two. The elder was old and blind, and I thought that he perhaps suffered from dementia. His son had died and today was the funeral. There was to be a big ceremony. All the villagers turned out to place money in a pot for the family and I was paraded around, a curiosity to be ogled. The number-two chief told me I was the first white person they'd seen in the village for ten years and, at all times, men of authority accompanied me. This was not a gesture of respect. This was a precaution, to ensure that nothing bad happened to me. The villagers radiated a mix of curiosity and hostility. I was taken to a football match that ended in a mass brawl. Violence was obviously commonplace, and the men in authority wanted to monitor it. If that hostility remained unchecked, and I came to harm, nobody would get paid.

There were no facilities to charge my phone, so I had no means of keeping in contact with the guys. It was only later that I learned what they'd been up against. When they received the call to say that I was in Sumbi, they tried to rent motorbikes of their own but got scammed. They managed to drive the van a very long way round to a village called Tshela, but the most direct route from Tshela to Sumbi was through deep jungle, which required a four-by-four. They approached the police chief. In a village like Tshela, the police chief is not quite the official we would imagine the title to confer in the West. He was just a guy with a few more bits and bobs than the other villagers, and no qualms about using them to earn himself a little money. He had a beaten-up old four-by-four, which he loaned to the guys for $500. They couldn't just take it, however. The police chief insisted that he provide a driver and a mechanic, because the chances of this clapped-out vehicle making it all the way through the jungle to Sumbi were vanishingly small, and this too came at a cost. The guys had no option but to accept these terms, and they finally arrived at midnight on my second night in Sumbi.

I was relieved to see them. More relieved than I can say. But I was also angry. Angry with myself, and angry with us as a team. Now that I felt safe – or at least safer – I was able to analyse our decisions over the past few days. I'd been terribly naïve in thinking that our van was up to the task of navigating the route we had chosen through the DRC. A quick look at the satellite imagery would have told me which roads were tarmacked – and therefore passable – and which roads weren't. They say that if you fail to plan, you plan to fail. That's what I'd done. Perhaps more importantly, we'd failed to establish a proper contingency plan for an event like this. When the stakes were high, and we didn't know, either literally or metaphorically, what the road ahead held, and we understood the consequences of getting kidnapped in the DRC, hindsight made it obvious that we should have returned to the tarmac and tried to regroup. The decision to have people take me to Sumbi – a day's travel away – and hope that somehow we'd muddle our way through from there made no sense to me. I blamed myself for not establishing proper emergency procedures and, not for the first time, I wondered if we as a team had all the skills we required to complete this mission.

We paid the money that the big dogs of the village expected – it amounted to a few hundred dollars – and the next morning we piled into the beaten-up four-by-four and headed back along the jungle trails to Tshela. The way back took us through a number of poor villages. At one point the four-by-four broke down and the mechanic told us we needed to buy more brake fluid at an inflated price. I knew he was exaggerating the cost, but we had no option but to pay it, and as we waited in this village for the repairs to be done, the tensions in the team worsened. The guys bought cigarettes and beer and sat smoking and drinking while we waited. It was understandable: the past couple of days had been profoundly stressful for them, and they needed some way to unwind. It sat badly with me, however. Naked kids with bellies bloated from malnutrition played in the dirt all around us. There were families clearly unable to afford food and clothes. For us white boys to be sitting around with beers and fags was not only a bad look, it was a dangerous look. We were flaunting our money in front of people who had none, and I wanted it to stop.

We argued. Badly. All the frustrations and anxieties I had about our abilities as a team came out. And so did all the complicated emotions I'd experienced over the past few days. I felt the others had absolutely no idea what I'd been through or what I thought would happen to me. I realise now that they probably felt the same. Our experience in the DRC had been so terribly difficult for every individual on the team that we'd all been pushed to the very extremes of our stress tolerance. The guys thought I was over-reacting. I thought they lacked empathy for what I'd endured. In fact, we had all been under so much pressure that we couldn't see matters from anyone else's perspective. We were all right, and we were all wrong.

I returned to the four-by-four and sat in it, waiting for the repairs to be finished. Back on the road, a frosty atmosphere descended, and it continued to surround us back in the village of Tshela. The police chief invented some bogus reasons why we owed him more money than he'd previously quoted, and of course we had no option but to pay him. The whole episode had cost us several thousand dollars that the mission could ill afford, and although our safety was more important than money, it was a blow, especially in the wake of the armed robbery in Angola.

The next day we had a team meeting. I felt so disrespected that I lost my cool and threw a chair. Clearly the stresses had accumulated. Clearly none of us were dealing with them well. Clearly something had to change.

Our main focus was to continue the mission and get out of the DRC as quickly as possible. We drove the van back to the start point of Day 102 and plotted a new route. It was evident that the direct route north towards the border with the Republic of the Congo was impassable for us. We had two options. The first was to follow a main road to the capital of Kinshasa. It lies on the Congo River. On the other side of the river is the city of Brazzaville, which lies in the Republic of the Congo. There was, however, no bridge. To cross there would have meant me taking a boat, which would have been cheating. So we decided on our second option: to head west, along roads which we knew to be tarmacked, to the Angolan exclave of Cabinda. It meant a detour of many hundreds of kilometres, but really we had no other choice.

Back on the road, I had time to think. After a couple of days of running, I sat the boys down and I apologised. I apologised for losing my cool. I apologised for being so blunt with everyone. I apologised for not understanding the strain they'd been under. I became emotional as I explained to them that I thought I was going to die when I was on that motorbike, but I regretted not taking the time to consider what they'd been through. I told them that I realised I'd been asking too much of them, and providing too little support. And I told them that I had a plan going forwards.

The inability of our van to cope with the terrain we'd encountered had been a major factor in our troubles in the DRC. Something had to be done about it. I had recently signed a deal to write the book you are now reading. It meant I had a little bit of money that I could use to buy a four-by-four. To ease the guys' unrealistic workload, I decided to hire two more team members: one to help Harry with logistics, one to help Stan with content. And I explained that I wanted Harry, Jarred and Stan to each take a month's holiday, because they hadn't had a break since the beginning of the mission, and they needed it. We would organise all this when we reached Cabinda.

My suggestions were, I think, well received. A little heat left the situation. A guy called George who worked in the DRC had reached out on Instagram to offer us accommodation in a former British and French special forces compound, so we had a secure base that mitigated some of the dangers and eased our anxiety levels. It felt good for the team dynamics to be, to some extent, back to where they were. And as the terrain became more open and the Cabinda border approached, I felt a little safer. We still had the occasional encounter with officials on the make, we still experienced hostility from passers-by, but our route had become a little less sketchy.

As we approached the border with Cabinda, the tarmac road deteriorated again and I endured some of the toughest running yet, on winding tracks of deep sand that felt like wading through treacle and badly blistered my feet. I only managed 37 kilometres on Day 110, and they were some of the hardest kilometres of the mission. But the following day we finally crossed over the border.

We weren't sorry to leave the DRC behind. We'd only briefly tasted the difficulties of life in that country, and the trauma of my experiences would remain with me for a long time. In the weeks that followed, even though the events of that night were in the past, I relived them often. From time to time, as I ran, the memories would hit me and I'd feel like I was about to have a heart attack. A visceral, physical reaction to the most terrifying few hours of my life. That experience was behind me, but even now I find it harrowing to recall. Sometimes I wonder if it will ever leave me.

16

ANXIOUS GEEZER

Cabinda is part of Angola, and we'd grown accustomed to Angola. After the dangers of the DRC, it felt good to be back in that country. Like a home from home. There was a large expat community and, because of the friends and contacts we'd made in Angola, as soon as it became known that we were heading into the exclave, offers of help and accommodation rolled in. We stayed our first night in a proper hotel and ate in a restaurant. We found someone to do running repairs to the van. And we turned our attention to my new plan, and the purchase of a four-by-four.

The state of the roads in the DRC had persuaded me that we needed a new vehicle, but in fact the decision went some way to solving a problem that had been on my mind for some time. We had always known that our route north would take us through the Republic of the Congo and into Cameroon and then Nigeria. We'd been warned that parts of Cameroon were unstable and dangerous to visit, and that the border with Nigeria posed problems. Certain stretches of that border were closed and other stretches were in areas too unstable to visit. Our best bet was to cross a mountainous border region. This would be tough running, involving many thousands of metres of ascent. But as hard as it would be for me, it would be impossible for the van. Our working strategy had been that a couple of the guys would put the van on a boat to meet us in Nigeria, while I and one other paid some locals to support us across the mountain range with motorbikes. Hardly ideal. A four-by-four, however, would be able to cross the mountainous terrain. We'd still have to put the van on a boat, but at least we would not then be reliant on the help of others.

We spent ten days in Cabinda while repairs were done to the van. The idea of no rest days had of course set sail by this point, so I spent the time doing some weights and putting back on some of the bulk that I'd lost. Harry went on holiday, with the plan that he would rejoin us in about a month in Yaoundé, the capital of Cameroon. When Harry returned, the plan was for Jarred to go on holiday until we reached Lagos, Nigeria. And after that, Stan would go on holiday until we reached Abidjan in Ivory Coast.

I put out an advert to recruit two new team members. I wanted someone who'd had a lot of experience travelling through Africa and was well versed in the logistical challenges involved. And I wanted another video editor who could take the pressure off Stan, who, between shooting all day and editing all night, had too much work to do. Lots of people applied for the roles, from all round the world. I asked Stan to make a shortlist of those applicants he thought had the correct editing experience, and I then filtered the shortlist based on personality. I finally settled on a young man in his mid-twenties called Jamie, born in the UK but living in Germany.

In terms of the logistics job, I decided quite quickly that Guus van Veen was the guy for us. He'd been a paratrooper in the

Dutch military and had spent two years cycling around the world, which included the route from Egypt to South Africa and then back up to Chad. He'd spent time in African prisons and was fully aware of the challenges involved in overlanding the continent. He was a year younger than me, and spoke English, Dutch, French, German and a bit of Portuguese. He was big and strong, physically a presence. When I spoke to him for the first time he was in the Netherlands, but had only recently returned from Africa and was keen to get back.

We agreed that Guus would meet us in a couple of weeks' time, once he'd sorted out all his visas. Jamie would join us in Cameroon.

It was too expensive to buy a four-by-four in Cabinda. We looked into getting one shipped out from the UK, but it would have taken too long. We decided to buy one in South Africa and have a friend of Jarred's drive it up through the continent to us. A straightforward idea in principle. When Jarred's friend inadvertently drove it under a height-restriction barrier and smashed up the bonnet, the A frame and the windscreen, I realised that it perhaps wouldn't be quite such a straightforward idea in practice. We managed to get it fixed up, but that and other delays meant we also wouldn't take delivery of the four-by-four until we were in Cameroon. No matter. The van would suffice until then.

We hadn't originally expected to find ourselves in Cabinda. Now that we were here, however, we planned to head north, across the border to the town of Pointe-Noire in the Republic of the Congo, or ROC. From there we planned to head north into the country of Gabon, which had never been part of our itinerary, but now offered the most direct route to Cameroon.

I was itching to get back on the road. In reality, we could have done with a few more days in Cabinda to tie up various loose ends, but all I wanted to do was start running again. As soon as the van was fixed, Stan, Jarred and I hit the road and headed north to the border. I didn't know much about the ROC. I didn't know how it compared to the DRC, although I'd heard that, like most countries in this region, it had encountered its difficulties with political unrest and corruption. So I approached it nervously.

We crossed the border as the light was failing and decided to find somewhere to camp for the night. Within half an hour, our van got stuck in a sand road. We had to find some locals to help pull us out. They took us to a nearby hotel, where we overnighted in the car park. The next day we went back to the border so I could begin my run. As I started the ones and twos, a dreadful sense of impending doom crashed over me. I'd never had a panic attack before, so I couldn't say for certain if I was having one now, but it felt as I imagined a heart attack would feel. I was experiencing overwhelming anxiety at being away from the perceived safety of Cabinda. Having escaped the situation in the DRC, I didn't know what awaited me in the ROC, and I didn't know if we as a team had the skills to deal with it.

Panic attacks aside, we arrived in Pointe-Noire in decent shape and prepared to continue north into Gabon. At exactly that moment, however, there was civil unrest in Gabon and the borders were closed. From our perspective it was a good job that the coup happened when it did. Had we been in-country at the time, we'd have been in trouble. As it was, we altered our plans once more and decided to head east to the city of Brazzaville.

We dealt with our anxiety, over those first few days in the ROC, with humour. We shared crazy, laddish jokes in a slightly unhinged attempt to divert our attention from our worries. We just wanted to shock ourselves into laughter and distract ourselves from the fear. It turned out, though, that the ROC was nothing like the DRC. In fact, from my perspective, it was the most chill of all the central African countries. The road to Brazzaville was beautiful – surrounded by verdant jungle terrain – but, crucially for me, well tarmacked. The ROC hosts a large population of Chinese migrants, and Chinese companies had constructed a major new road between Pointe-Noire and Brazzaville. Good for the ROC, good for me. I'd learned to appreciate asphalt.

We'd had an extended break in Cabinda, but extended breaks meant that my body had to reacclimatise itself to the punishment of daily ultramarathons. As I strode out on the asphalt from Pointe-Noire, my foot started to swell. No ordinary swelling. I could barely step on it without an agonising stab, and I had to cut holes in my shoes to relieve the pressure. A doctor would have told me to stop running immediately, of course, but I just couldn't afford to lose any more time. And anyway, I knew now that the best way to deal with these issues was to push on through them. The swelling failed to improve, however. Each step shot fireworks of pain up my leg. I allowed myself to walk certain stretches, and for a couple of weeks I only managed to clock up a single marathon a day. Each night I would smear ibuprofen gel over the swelling and, if possible, ice it – although ice was hard to come by. The swelling would ease off overnight, but as soon as I started running it would worsen again. I simply had to rely on my implicit faith that things would work themselves out. My foot was inflamed because I'd chucked a load of mileage at it again. Instead of stopping, I reduced the mileage to a point where the injury levelled out rather than getting worse every day, and hovered around that sweet spot until things started to improve. The strategy worked, but it slowed me down.

And then we hit another bump in the road.

A couple of hours outside Brazzaville, the van broke down yet again. It was the clutch this time. We called a mechanic in the city who wanted the equivalent of £1,000 to come and tow us. We didn't have that kind of money, so we decided to see if a passing vehicle might agree to tow us for less. Sure enough, a guy with an old four-by-four took the job. Unfortunately, his vehicle broke down every 20 minutes, so what should have been a two-hour tow turned into a 16-hour epic. After stopping for dinner, the driver started towing us again before we were ready and pulled us into the path of a moving truck. It nearly totalled the van. The window was shattered, the doors wouldn't shut on either side, the bonnet was mangled. In the UK it would unquestionably have been a write-off. Not in Africa. We took it to some mechanics who worked on it for a week and did a pretty good job refitting the windscreen with Plexiglass, remoulding the metal and, of course, fixing the clutch. Good news that the van kind of worked; bad news that it meant another week's delay.

The city of Brazzaville lies across the Congo River from the city of Kinshasa in the DRC. On a satellite map it looks like a single city divided by the river, but the two places couldn't be more different. The population of Kinshasa is 17 million, whereas the population of Brazzaville is less than 2 million. No bridge connects them. They are distinct and separate. In a straight line, Brazzaville is less than 600 kilometres from Luanda, the capital of Angola. Because of all our hindrances and detours, it had taken us several weeks to get here. By any measure, we'd gone the long way round. At this rate of progress, the mission could easily take two years. I decided that from that point on, I would make a special effort to crack as much mileage as I could every day. I would raise my game.

Our stay in Brazzaville coincided with the arrival of one of our new teammates: Guus. I immediately knew that he would be a positive influence on our mission. I'd grown to understand that a team like this, attempting a mission like this, required a leader and a hierarchy. So far, I had not been a strong leader. It meant that any hierarchy within the team had dissolved. Guus, though, was a military man. He was accustomed to rank. He treated me as the leader of the mission, and this had a subtle but distinct knock-on effect on me, and on the team as a whole.

As soon as Guus hooked up with us, I told him that his number-one job was to work out how we were going to cross the Cameroon–Nigeria border, because we knew the van would struggle with it. He got straight on it. Our second team member, Jamie, had not yet joined us. He would arrive in Brazzaville later, take delivery of the four-by-four from Jarred's mate, who by then would have driven it from South Africa, and drive it north in time for us to use it to cross the border between Cameroon and Nigeria.

The road from Brazzaville north to Ouesso, near the Cameroonian border, was much like the road from Pointe-Noire – Chinese-built and newly tarmacked. It meant, now that the swelling in my foot had subsided, that I could go back to 60 kilometres a day, which I did for that entire stretch. Guus was an early riser, so I'd be up at 6am every morning to put in the ones and twos. Any anxieties I'd had about the ROC were unfounded. We passed unhindered through a series of villages where the people were extremely friendly and welcoming. Most importantly, we felt safe. My only real obstacles on the stretch between Brazzaville and Cameroon were the bugs and the rain. The hot, humid air was thick with flies and midges and all manner of insects that I didn't recognise, some of them the size of golf balls, like mini dinosaurs buzzing around and biting. Swarming around me everywhere I went, their bites caused huge welts on my skin, although I didn't get it so bad as the other guys. I don't know why – maybe it was because I was moving around more. Still, it was horrible to have them dive-bombing me every day. I couldn't get free of them, apart from when the rain fell.

Because when the rain fell, everyone and everything sought shelter. Except me.

We'd barely seen any rain since South Africa. Here, for a couple of hours a day, we experienced rainfall so heavy that I couldn't have been wetter if I'd been running in the shower. I quite enjoyed the rain. It offered relief from the heat, the humidity and the insects, and it forced me into a more ferocious mentality. You couldn't plod along through those conditions. You had to attack them. The downpours forced every other road user inside, and would temporarily flood the road. I'd end up running alone through a river of rain, jaw clenched, trainers squelching, beard dripping, determined to put in the miles.

A certain monotony set in, and although monotony was preferable to danger, I think I suffered from mental exhaustion. My enthusiasm waned for talking to camera and taking part in the creation of our content. There were fun moments on the journey – at one point we bought a dwarf crocodile from some villagers and kept it for a couple of days before releasing it back into the wild – but I struggled at times with my motivation. I understand now how important it was that I had to think about matters other than running, such as logistics and my relationship with the team. If the situation had been more like the Asia to London run, when I was almost always alone and really I only had to think about myself, I'm certain that my psychological state would have quickly unravelled in the ROC. I couldn't afford to become too inward-looking.

And so I learned something important on that stretch of the run, as I struggled with my mindset and reflected on the value of being there for and with my companions. One of the main purposes of living is to be of service to other people. I'd jogged round the outskirts of this realisation as I began to understand the importance of community in the poor villages of Angola, but as the solitary miles passed beneath my feet in the ROC, I thought more about the importance of our relationships with others. It struck me that the times in my life when I'd ended up simply thinking about myself had been the hardest. Caught up in my own worries, concerned only with my own welfare or lack of it, I had spiralled. I might have spiralled now, if there hadn't been others on the road with me. Because when you have to show up, when you have to work as part of a team and think about the concerns and needs of other people, it gives your mindset the impetus not to deteriorate. By no means did I – or have I – perfected this way of thinking. At many times, on the road in Africa and since, I've found myself getting caught up in my own head. But it never leads me down the right path, and I was grateful for my team in those days. They saw me through.

17

MOUNTAIN GEEZER

I was sad to leave the Republic of the Congo. After the delays and stresses of Angola and the DRC, we'd made good progress there. Swollen limbs and smashed-up vans aside, it had been relatively straightforward. I had to keep on smashing the tarmac, though, which meant crossing over into our next country: Cameroon. We did this on Day 163.

If you look at a map, you'll see that much of the border between ROC and Cameroon is a straight line, as though drawn with a ruler by a guy in an office, which it probably was. In reality it's thick, primary jungle. The crossing was straightforward, despite the astonishment of the Cameroonian border officials when we told them the details of our mission. And on first impression there appeared to be no great alteration in terrain or infrastructure in comparison to the ROC. A transition rather than a hard change. Gradually, though, it became apparent that our route was taking us through larger villages with bigger buildings. It felt somehow more prosperous than the ROC.

We knew that the western part of Cameroon was unsettled, but we expected the area around the border with the ROC to be relatively safe and secure, and so it was. Our various nationalities

– English, Dutch and South African – helped. One day, as we were hanging out by the bus on the side of the road, a couple of guys on motorbikes pulled up. They didn't give off the hostile vibes that we experienced in the DRC – nothing like – but equally they didn't immediately give the impression of welcoming us to their country. They spoke to Guus in French and I could tell they weren't happy. Guus explained to us that they thought we might be French. When they realised we weren't, they backed off. Cameroon had been colonised by Germany. After the First World War, it was divided between British and French rule. Clearly the memories and resentments of that colonisation remained, and the French had earned themselves a worse reputation than the British, although I'd no idea why that should have been the case. It worried me that our next country was Nigeria, also formerly colonised by the British. I wondered what kind of reception we'd have there.

Harry was due to rejoin us in Yaoundé, the capital of Cameroon. With a couple of weeks to go, however, he called to say that he had to delay his return for personal reasons. I arranged a temporary replacement – James, who would join us in Nigeria. By the time Harry was ready to rejoin us, however, I felt that Guus was completely on top of all our logistics. It cost the mission several thousand pounds a month of its dwindling funds to have another teammate, so I had to break the news to Harry that I wasn't going to ask him to return. He was understandably upset. Harry had been with us from the very beginning, an integral part of that early team. We'd shared some difficult experiences together, but I was learning that leadership sometimes required me to make tough decisions according to what I thought best for the mission. From a personal point of view, I'd have loved Harry to come back. I had to put my personal preferences to one side, however, no matter how unpalatable I found it.

There were other unpalatable moments to come. One day, I bought an egg omelette by the side of the road. Bad move. That night, in a basic hotel in a little Cameroonian village, I spent the entire night on the toilet. Food poisoning, which had been such a problem for me in Namibia, had hit again. I'd run through it last time, though, and I had no intention of letting a bout of the runs stop me this time round. So I hit the road and I managed five kilometres, still shitting and puking. I decided to take the rest of the day off. The following day I ran again. Having pushed on through episodes of dehydration and near-delirium once already, I knew I could do it again.

I also knew, however, how my body had reacted to that punishment last time round. I'd started pissing blood, and those symptoms had only eased when I'd stopped running for a couple of days. Now the symptoms returned. My urine turned red again. I was done with delays, however. I didn't want to take any rest days no matter what my body was telling me. I knew there was no point going to a doctor, because he'd only tell me to stop running. I'd recently been smashing 60-kilometre days, so I decided I'd just ease off the mileage and bring it down to 50 while I waited for things to return to normal down below. The guys didn't try to persuade me otherwise. They knew I'd made up my mind, and that I wanted to keep forward momentum at all costs.

Our new team member, Jamie, joined us as we approached the border with Nigeria. He had with him our new toy: the long-awaited four-by-four. As support vehicles go, it was pretty sweet: a double bed, loads of storage, cooking facilities and even a shower hose. Most importantly, though, it could cross terrain that we couldn't even consider in the van. And our terrain became more hilly as we started to penetrate the mountainous region in the north-west of the country. The hills made for tough running, especially as I was still pissing blood. As we gained altitude, though, the temperature and humidity diminished and my health improved. By Day 178, my piss was clear and I felt ready to tackle the next stage of the mission.

Our old van would not be able to cross the mountain pass between Cameroon and Nigeria. Only the four-by-four could do that. Jarred was by now taking the holiday I'd prescribed, so this was the plan: Jamie and Stan would drive the van to the coast, put it on a boat and cross the Gulf of Guinea to meet us in Nigeria. Their route had the advantage of not having to deal with the treacherous road conditions, but it had the disadvantage of crossing the most pirate-infested waters in the world. So: swings and roundabouts. The sea voyage was no good for me, because it would, of course, mean that I would fail to run for a stretch of the route. Instead, Guus and I would take the four-by-four over the mountains. So we said goodbye to Jamie and Stan and continued the journey as a duo.

As we approached the mountain range, a couple of heavily armed policemen stopped us. The way ahead, they said, was too dangerous. The risk of terrorism was too high. We weren't to continue. Not continuing, of course, wasn't an option. We managed to talk our way past them and keep going on our journey, but the incident kept us mindful of the potential dangers ahead. And maybe that mountain region did present a danger of terrorism. If so, we were fortunate enough not to encounter it. By far our biggest obstacle, as expected, was the terrain.

These were steep mountain paths without a crumb of tarmac in sight. I had to climb mountains' worth of ascent every day without the benefit of anything firm underfoot. The biggest day was 1,500 metres of ascent, more than the height of Ben Nevis. Even with that elevation I maintained my daily target of between 50 and 60 kilometres. The roads themselves badly deteriorated. In fact, they were barely roads at all. Loose stones. Loose mud. Rivers without bridges that needed crossing. I'd run straight through the water and Guus would plough the torrent in the four-by-four. Before long, the four-by-four setting broke, so it was only running on two-by-four, rear-wheel drive. Guus was a skilled driver, but the vehicle frequently got stuck. Locals in the mountain villages often had to help dig us out of ditches. I was comfortably faster than the truck.

We ran through some of the tiniest, most rural villages I'd seen. Little more than wooden shacks with no access from a proper tarmacked road. Extreme poverty. Now and then, a huge, ancient lorry that was designed for this terrain would bring supplies to the villages, but they still had very little to live on, and sourced their water from rivers. Despite the challenges, though, it was perhaps the most beautiful part of the mission, and the slight drop in temperature and humidity was a welcome relief. You take the positives where you can.

The border crossing into Nigeria was one of the least official we'd experienced. Ordinarily, the border posts for each country would be separated by a no man's land of about a hundred metres. Here, I had to run about five kilometres from the Cameroonian post to the Nigerian post. We crossed these sparsely manned posts without any trouble. When the Nigerian border guard saw that I was English, he yelled out: 'You're my grandfather!' So much for my concerns about anti-British feeling in this former colony.

Stan and Jamie, meanwhile, had a more torrid time of it. Delayed for days, they finally managed to get the van on a boat. All they had to do now was avoid the threat of pirates. Or so they thought. As it turned out, pirates weren't their problem.

The weather was their problem.

They stowed the van on an overloaded old wooden boat and set sail – only to be hit by a massive thunderstorm. They thought it was game over. The storm was so violent that Jamie texted his mum, thinking he was going to die. You can imagine their relief when they finally made it safely to land.

• • •

While the foothills of the mountain range in Nigeria were rural and really quite beautiful, it was a relief to be back on the tarmac. As we headed west in the direction of Lagos, however, we had the sense that our route was becoming a little more dangerous again. We started to encounter checkpoints on the road. These would be manned by up to 20 police officers in military uniform carrying rifles. It was impossible to predict whether they'd be welcoming or obstructive. Sometimes they'd wave us past. Sometimes they'd hold us up, demand to see our documents and ask questions. And sometimes these checkpoints were not manned by police officers at all, but by a random bunch of lads whose aim was to extort money out of anybody they could. Occasionally these unofficial checkpoints would be situated alongside the official ones, and the lads in their civvies would try, unsuccessfully, to rob us in full view of the police. On a few occasions I asked the police why they allowed this to happen. They shrugged it off. 'They're not bad people.' 'They're just helping the police out.' From time to time an official policeman would subcontract his work out to some guys while he sat back and chilled out all day. It became hard to distinguish between genuine checkpoints and bandits out to rob us.

Compared to Guus in the truck, I attracted a little less attention when I was on foot, as I less obviously carried anything of value. Sometimes I'd be asked for my passport. Sometimes I'd be asked for money. I'd had enough experience of these demands by now that I could confidently bat them back. 'I'm showing you nothing until you show me your badge. And I'm not giving you any money.' I was always wary of handing over my passport, because I knew that once I'd done that, they really could demand anything they wanted. Sometimes it got me into trouble, as the checkpoint geezers would crowd round with their mates, trying to intimidate me. They would invent bogus laws on the spot, or over-zealously apply existing rules to us that they routinely overlooked for others.

Guus was held for several hours at a checkpoint for not wearing his seatbelt, while vans sped past with seven blokes hanging out of them. They would claim that, as we were Europeans, we were being held to a higher standard. On one occasion we were taken to a police station, to be fined for the misdemeanour of having a four-by-four with the steering on the wrong side. Up in front of the police chief and his number two, we could tell that they were peeved that the lower-ranked police officers had thought we were worth troubling with, but on that occasion we had no option but to pay our fine.

Despite the occasional aggro we encountered at these checkpoints, I quickly grew to like Nigeria and its people. Part of it was because English was widely spoken, as it meant that, for the first time since Namibia, I was able to converse freely with people I met. Even when people tried it on with me, they did it with a twinkle in their eye. By and large they were hustlers, and there was something almost endearing about the way they went about it.

The temperature in Nigeria was the hottest we'd yet experienced, regularly over 40 degrees, with terrible humidity. I maintained my 60-kilometre days, and even upped it to 65 or 70 kilometres on occasion. It was on this stretch of the mission, however, that I encountered perhaps the most extreme effect on my health so far.

Relentless uphill running presents unique challenges to your body. When you're running on the flat, you only have to lift your foot a certain amount to take a step. On an incline, you have to lift it higher. This puts a huge strain on the hip flexors. There had been rolling hills throughout the ROC and Cameroon, such that I'd often manage to accumulate 800–900 metres of ascent in the course of a day's running. My hip flexors were already being asked to work hard. This mountain range along the Cameroon–Nigeria border, however, asked too much of them. I'd felt a few twinges in my back as I'd been running, but I didn't pay them too much notice. Such twinges were commonplace. It's impossible to run daily ultramarathons without a whole range of niggles presenting themselves. My strategy would always be simply to run through those niggles. Invariably they'd sort themselves out.

These twinges, though, did not sort themselves out. They got worse. As I ran through Nigeria, pain would shoot down my legs and my back would seize up to the extent that, if I was sitting, I wouldn't be able to stand. Forget about bending down. The symptoms would come and go, lulling me into a false sense of security. One minute I'd be fine, the next I'd be in unspeakable pain, barely able to move. It felt as if someone had a remote control and could press a button to make me seize up. I had no agency over the matter. The pain would kick in whether I was resting or running. I'd look behind to check for traffic and my back would go. My leg would collapse in on itself, like a puppet with a cut string. At night I couldn't sleep from the pain. More than any other injury – the food poisoning, the pissing blood, the swollen joints and limbs – it was this one that felt as if it had the potential to completely derail the mission. The pain was so intense that it prevented me from thinking about anything else.

Stopping wasn't an option. I brought my mileage down from the 65–70-kilometre range to the 40–50 range. The pain didn't only affect my body, though. It also affected my mind. I'd been running the length of Africa for the best part of 200 days and I was exhausted. Completely spent. The idea of running thousands more kilometres with this level of pain and unable to control the flexibility and movement of my body demoralised me. I didn't quite lose hope that I would finish the mission, but I found it hard to see the light at the end of the tunnel. I'd exhausted all my little motivational mind games, like dividing the day into manageable sections, and I found it hard to put a positive spin on the situation. There was no gallows humour. I'd reached the limit of what I could tolerate. I had to come to terms with the fact that this mission was far, far more difficult than I ever expected. I can offer no pretty, motivational insights from that time. I could only rely on my bloody-mindedness, and on the knowledge that if I stopped now, the 200 days of running that I'd already put in would all be for nothing.

• • •

After a small delay caused by putting the wrong type of fuel into the van, Stan and Jamie rejoined us in the vicinity of Enugu after their treacherous journey by sea. I continued to run through the pain until one day when I found that I couldn't even sit up in my bunk. I decided that the time had come to speak to somebody who knew what they were talking about. I took a day off to have video calls with a bunch of physios in the UK. It was hard for any of them to be certain what the problem was without examining me, but one guy explained to me about the hip flexors. He thought they'd pulled my pelvis and spine a bit tight, resulting in a nerve issue. He advised that I slightly alter my running form and drop the intensity for a while. If I did that, the pain should start easing off.

I did as I was told. I dropped the intensity and for a few days I even walked instead of running. It helped. A bit. Then I cranked it up again. I only averaged 45 to 50 kilometres a day, and that lower mileage persisted for the next three months, until I hit Mauritania. The pain returned, so I treated the symptoms with strong painkillers and sleeping tablets. These were available over the counter at Nigerian pharmacists, but they were serious drugs. The painkillers gave me a fuzzy feeling that I liked a bit too much. The sleeping pills stopped me waking up at night in agony. These were not the type of medicines that you're supposed to take for long periods of time, but I ignored the instructions on the packet in the interest of keeping my mileage up. I kept popping the pills.

Nigeria has one of the most developed economies in Africa. Unlike in the previous few countries we'd visited, we could visit shops that sold only products made in Nigeria, rather than imported from Europe. It meant that there was a lower financial barrier to entry for slightly more luxurious foods. In Angola and the Congo, you could eat cheaply enough if you ate like a local, which normally meant eating cassava root and pap, with little or no meat. As soon as you tried to buy luxury items like bread or biscuits, it became very expensive very quickly. Not so in Nigeria – although there was also a market in expensive, high-end products for the very rich, which tells you something about the country. It's not a poor economy, but the gap between rich and poor is extreme. There is phenomenal wealth, but millions live in hunger and without certain dignities we take for granted. I was running in the vicinity of Lagos one day, along a busy road in an industrial area full of traffic. The fumes were thick and choking. There was no hard shoulder so I was forever having to jump out of the way of trucks that refused to give me a metre's clearance. Sensory overload. From time to time, wing mirrors would nick my arm and my legs were covered in tiny cuts from where I'd had to jump into bushes to avoid being hit. On this particular day I saw something lying by the side of the road up ahead. As I approached, I realised it wasn't some*thing* after all. It was some*one*: a dead man, abandoned and alone. He lay face up with his eyes closed, and he'd obviously been there for some time, because his skin had turned from brown to a charred black colour in the brutal heat. He wore ragged clothing and was wasting away. Flies crawled over his skin.

I didn't linger. As I ran off, I reflected on how he hadn't seemed like an old man. His early, undignified death was presumably simply a result of his poverty. His fate was probably not so different to the potential fate of hundreds of people I'd seen on my journey so far. It put my own troubles and aspirations into perspective. So many millions of people on the continent of Africa – and indeed around the world – worried daily about matters of life and death. It made my mission seem a bit silly, in the grand scheme of things. My back hurt, the road was hard, I felt sorry for myself, but really: things could be worse. I could be that guy, or many like him.

As I ran through the crazy, crowded city of Lagos, people shouted '*Oyinbo*' at me as I passed. It's a Nigerian term for people of European descent. Was it friendly or hostile? A bit of both, and sometimes hard to tell.

Lagos is a vast, sprawling place, one of the many big cities I would run through as our route took us through West Africa. This is where most of the opportunities are on the continent. It's where people congregate. So far, my route through Africa had been almost entirely rural. Now I had to get used to the hot, noisy bustle of West African cities. There was money here, for sure, but the brutal juxtaposition of rich and poor was evident. The city was polluted, there was rubbish everywhere. I breathed car fumes and dodged puddles of raw sewage in the street. I'd finish each day covered with grime. There were skyscrapers and vast slums and sketchy checkpoints manned by bogus guards. There was poverty and there was bling.

I noticed that far more people had smartphones than had been the case elsewhere – another indication that this was an economically more prosperous country. The Nigerians *loved* their smartphones and they *loved* their Snapchat, their Instagram and their other social media platforms. Being an unusual sight – a white man with a big orange beard running through their country – locals continually stopped me to ask for selfies. I'd have been happy just to put my head down and carry on running, but when the time came for me to leave, the Nigerian preoccupation with internet fame came in handy.

By the time I reached the Nigerian border, I'd overstayed my visa by a day. It meant that, as I tried to leave, I came up against resolute officialdom. Computer says no. A few hours passed, and it looked like they were prepared for a few more hours to pass too. And so I did something I'd never done before. I pulled out my phone and brought up an article on the BBC website about me and the mission. It wasn't quite a 'do you know who I am?' moment, but I guess it wasn't far off. It was a bit of a flex and worth a try if it got us more quickly through the border. The Nigerian fondness for all things social media – and their respect for the hustle – worked its magic. The officials seemed pretty excited to see my face staring out at them from their phone, albeit somewhat bemused by the nature of my mission. They demanded photographs for their own social media. Happy to oblige, mate. After a few selfies we were the best of friends and I was allowed through.

I didn't particularly relish the strategy – I was running for reasons other than celebrity – but it solved a problem. And the game's the game. I was out of Nigeria and into Benin.

18

UNDERCOVER GEEZER

If, before my mission started, I'd been asked to rattle off the names of all the countries in Africa, I might have struggled with Benin, and its neighbour Togo. Sandwiched between Nigeria and Ghana, they are narrow at their southern tips. My route across both would only span a couple of hundred kilometres, so I did not expect to see a great deal of these two tiny tropical countries. As it turned out, it took longer than expected to tick them off the list. Under ordinary circumstances it would have been possible to cross Benin in a day or two, but my back was in a terrible state when we arrived, and I took a few days off in the hope that it would make things better. Stan went on holiday, as arranged. Jarred returned. On Day 217, I tried to run again, but my legs and back felt mashed up. After walking 18 kilometres – forward progress at any cost – I felt like I'd run 100.

There's a strong culture in Benin of voodoo and black magic. We went to a temple where people worshipped pythons. Maybe this alternative medicine would cure my broken body. It didn't, of course. The only cure was to stop running, but I had no intention of weasling out of the mission like that.

I was still heavily dosed up on pills to take the edge off the pain and keep my mileage up, but I realised that this was not a long-term solution to my problem. The fuzzy feeling they gave me meant I was becoming too dependent on them. I'd already increased the dosage far beyond the recommended level. This state of affairs couldn't continue all the way to Tunisia. To take that many painkillers until the end of the mission would be carnage, especially for someone with my personality type. So I decided, even though it would cause me more discomfort, to ease off the pills.

Sure enough, the back pain intensified. I readjusted my expectations. The pain would not stop the mission. It would simply be a question of how much more the mission would cost me, physically and emotionally. My only option was to get back on the road and deal with the pain as best I could. So I gritted my teeth, hit the tarmac again and, within a couple of days, crossed Benin and Togo along the Atlantic coast. On Day 220, it was time to cross into Ghana.

• • •

Every so often we would meet other travellers on the road, often Europeans who were overlanding Africa, following a similar route to ours, only inverted. It takes a certain type of character to attempt such a journey, so these people were always worth talking to. On one occasion we met a Portuguese couple who had bundled their three children into the back of their car for an overlanding adventure – a pretty cool parenting choice, if you ask me. Other travellers would have sick ex-military vehicles that they'd converted to cope with the varied terrain. We'd chat with members of this strange, friendly community and share with them our experiences of the countries they had yet to visit, giving them tips about the terrain, the culture and the potential hazards. We'd warn them about the mountain pass between Nigeria and Cameroon. We'd tell them to take care in the DRC. And they'd do the same for us. We heard rumours of poor roads and dodgy internet in Guinea, and we heard that Ivory Coast was a fun place to be. Nobody, of course, had taken the route through Algeria and Mauritania, and for good reason. To travel through Mauritania meant dealing with a thousand kilometres of desert without any roads, and the visa situation in Algeria, which had forced us to invert our route in the first place, remained problematic. The success of our mission still depended on sorting out our entry into Algeria, and we still had no solution for that particular issue. It remained a constant thought in the back of our minds.

The consensus, though, from all the other travellers that we met on the road, was that Ghana was sweet. They were right. Ghana felt safe. Relaxed. In Nigeria, there had always been the sense that things could quickly get spicy. The hustle and the bustle had an edge. I'd not spent long enough in Benin or Togo to fully form an opinion of those countries, but almost as soon as I set foot in Ghana, the vibe felt almost European. Familiar, somehow. There was KFC! They gave us free food. Small pleasures like that meant a lot. The Ghanaian roads and infrastructure are good, and there is a large expat community, mostly centred in the capital, Accra. They reached out to us when they knew we were on our way, and offered to take us out for food and provide us with accommodation.

In Accra, a bar even put on an event, advertising that the Hardest Geezer would be in attendance. A bunch of expats, Ghanaians and a few Nigerians turned up. It was a strange moment for me, because for the first time I could tell that people were visibly nervous to meet me. I did my best to be myself and put them at their ease, because I didn't really want people to think I was anything other than a lad from Worthing. Celebrity, however minor, felt uncomfortable. I'd have been much happier alone on the tarmac. That night I drank a few beers. I don't think I drank alcohol more than three times during the whole mission. Whenever I did, the effect was instant. A couple of cheeky ones after weeks of ultramarathons would leave the Hardest Geezer half cut, and even the tiniest amount of alcohol would make the next day's running much, much tougher.

And I didn't need anything to increase the difficulty of the running. My back was still bad. However, I'd massively reduced my painkiller intake and I'd tried to adjust my running style, pushing my hips forwards a little to reduce the impact on my hip flexors. It's hard, though, to change your technique when you've been running a certain way for thousands of kilometres, and my concentration would inevitably lapse as I settled back into my usual style. So, instead, I eased off the mileage. In Cameroon and Nigeria I'd been caning it up and down the mountains and averaging 70-kilometre days. From Lagos onwards, I reduced the intensity to only a marathon a day and it started to pay off a little bit. By no means was it perfect, but I started to sense a slight improvement. The pain became more manageable. It hurt, but it didn't hurt all day and all night. There were moments of respite.

Ghana felt like respite more generally too. It was way less busy than Nigeria, but English was still spoken, which made me feel a little more at home. People joined me on the road as I ran, and there was comfort in companionship. Comfort, too, in the knowledge that we were making headway. Over 7,000 kilometres still lay ahead, but there was a sense of momentum building as we'd ticked off several countries in quick succession.

Most of all, though, Ghana felt legitimately safe. The process of running through a safe country without having to worry about mountain passes, kidnappings or dodgy roadblocks gave me time to think more carefully about the upcoming issue of Algeria. We were no closer to solving the conundrum. Our best plan was to try to get residency in Mauritania, and then apply for a resident's visa in Nouakchott, the Mauritanian capital. It was a long shot. Probably too long. The Algerians simply didn't want Westerners crossing that border. Another option was more gangster. The Mauritania–Algeria border is porous. There were some checkpoints, but hundreds of kilometres of desert separated them. We could easily cross illegally. But if we were caught in Algeria without a visa, the mission wouldn't end at the northernmost point of Africa. It would end in an Algerian prison, and that was not an outcome any of us fancied. We sat down as a team to discuss the matter, without coming to any useful conclusion. As I ran, the thought crystallised in my mind that there were simply too many moving parts for us to go about our entry into Algeria by official means. I wondered if we were going to have to be a bit more rogue about it.

In Ghana, Jarred received bad news. His father had been very ill throughout the entire mission. Now the end was near for him. Word reached Jarred from his family that, if he wanted to see his dad for a final time, he needed to head home. Jarred told me this one morning as he drove me to the start point. We were all deeply focused on the mission, of course, but not to the extent that we couldn't distinguish between what was and wasn't important. Jarred's family needed him, and he needed to be with his family. Neither of us doubted that the right thing for him to do was to leave. It was tough for him and for all of us. Jarred had been with the mission from the very beginning and intended to be with us until the very end. But now he had to go, and he did not return until I reached the finish line.

Stan had gone on holiday in Benin and was not due to return until we reached Ivory Coast. It meant that my team now comprised Guus, Jamie and James. For the first time, I had none of my original crew with me. I missed them, of course, but there was also something refreshing about having new faces around me. And Guus had taken well to his logistics role, which meant that the border crossing between Ghana and Ivory Coast – the next country on our itinerary – was well planned in advance and took place without any difficulty.

As soon as I crossed the border, I noticed the hard language change between English-speaking Ghana and French-speaking Ivory Coast. Various local languages routinely transcended these borders, but this was not the case in terms of the languages of colonisation. My lack of French meant that inevitably I felt a little less at ease in Ivory Coast than in Ghana, but Guus spoke good French and it was his job to communicate with the locals. And like Ghana, this was a country with good roads, good infrastructure and a welcome feeling of security. The capital, Abidjan, still had an African feel to it, of course, but the tall skyscrapers, impressive bridges and visible middle class gave it a semi-Western vibe. I saw public rubbish and recycling bins for the first time since we'd set off: a sight we take for granted in the UK, but the importance of which I appreciated after seeing debris littering the streets of Lagos.

In Abidjan we set ourselves a challenge: James and Jamie would try to find the worst meal available in that city, while Guus and I tried to find the best. We ventured into the poshest restaurant I'd ever entered, and ate the most delicious meal I'd ever eaten. Abidjan was a very long way from the slums of South Africa or the impoverished villages of Angola. I certainly hadn't envisaged, at the start of the mission, that our path would take us somewhere like this. Africa is a continent of extremes and contradictions. It's not all mud huts. We in the West often fail to appreciate this.

Between Lagos and Abidjan I'd been averaging about a marathon a day, the terrain had been mostly flat as we hugged the coastline and I'd allowed myself some walking breaks. This reduced intensity paid dividends in terms of my body. My back felt much better as we left Abidjan, and so it was on this stretch that I managed the longest run of any day of the mission.

It wasn't my idea to run 110 kilometres in one day. Harry's temporary replacement, James, who had joined us in Nigeria, is a runner and Guus also rated himself as an endurance athlete, having done a lot of long-distance cycling. They'd had a bit of friendly back-and-forth about who could run the furthest. Now that James's time with us was coming to an end in Ivory Coast, he wanted to join me for a day's running. Together we completed 60 kilometres. Guus wanted to join us, but we couldn't all be out running together, because there would be nobody to drive the vehicles or deal with the logistics. He was keen, therefore, to show us all what he was made of and run with me on a different day. 'But I wouldn't want it to just be 60 kilometres,' he told me. 'If I'm going to run, I'll want to do at least 100.'

A hundred? That's a fair old stomp for somebody who hasn't been training hard. The furthest Guus had run before was 26 kilometres. But if he wanted to give it a go, I was up for it. 'You give me a number,' I said, 'and we'll do it.'

He thought for a moment. 'Let's start with 150,' he said.

'Sure,' I said. My back was sufficiently repaired that I reckoned I could have completed that distance, even if it wouldn't have been a lot of fun. Even so, I felt pretty comfortable in predicting that none of us was going to be running 150 kilometres in a day. It's a big ask. Half that distance is a big ask. You don't just roll out of bed and knock out a couple of marathons without some preparation.

Guus got up at 5am the next day to get cracking. I had no desire to make such an early start, so I let him go and gave him a good three-hour head start. And fair dos: he didn't give up. We ran all day. I stopped for my regular rests, to eat and drink. Guus stomped on through. I finally caught up with him after dark about 90 kilometres from the start point. I've never seen anybody in worse shape. He was walking along the side of the road, his legs barely working, his hips on the point of collapse as he clutched his back and side to keep everything working and aligned. I ran past him. 'You okay?' I said. 'How you doing?'

'Totally fine,' he said.

I wasn't going to give him any stick. Ninety kilometres, when you've only ever run 26, is no mean feat. He'd already done something pretty astonishing. I also knew he was a proud guy. He'd been mouthing off about completing 150 kilometres and it must have been becoming apparent to him that it was much easier said than done.

Midnight arrived. Guus passed the 100-kilometre mark. He half collapsed. He was barely able to walk. But he carried on going. I told James to drive close to him. He was in such a state that I knew there was a good chance he'd completely collapse or pass out rather than quit. I kept running up ahead, so I wasn't there to see the moment, at the 108-kilometre mark, that he just couldn't take another step. He became quite emotional, and when we finally got him back to the hotel room, we had to carry him up the stairs and give him a bucket to piss in because he couldn't make it to the toilet.

I was so impressed. Guus had bashed a hundred in one go, having only ever run a quarter of that distance before. I'd never seen anyone mess themselves up like that for no good reason. It was pretty cool – no matter that he couldn't drive the next day, or that it took him a week or two to fully recover from the ordeal. I'm always blown away when people push themselves to the very edge of what's possible for them, and Guus had done just that.

Sure, we were a bunch of young men with healthy egos showing off to each other. Sure, the only reason I ran 110 kilometres that day was to shut everyone else up. But there are many worse ways for young men to express their egos than by challenging themselves to achieve feats at the very edge of their ability.

• • •

James left us in Ivory Coast, and Stan returned from his holiday. James and I had got on very well on a personal level. I even offered to keep him on, even though it wasn't strictly necessary from the point of view of the mission. He, though, wanted to be home for Christmas, and who could blame him? We intended to be in Guinea for Christmas, and the word on the overlanders' grapevine was that this was not a place full of peace and goodwill to all mankind. Our route demanded that we cross it, however, and our road took us northwest towards that border. I'd started running at night again. We'd knocked this on the head earlier in the mission for reasons of security, but we felt safe here in Ivory Coast and the ability to run into the night meant I could increase my mileage again.

I was running after dark on Day 246 when I came to a police checkpoint. It wasn't my first checkpoint. It wouldn't be my last. And even though Ivory Coast had a far more advanced infrastructure than some of the countries I'd travelled through, the checkpoints were ramshackle by European standards. Back home, an official security post would have proper buildings, signage and barriers. This checkpoint was a tiny shack with a tin roof and a couple of logs rolled across the road to stop cars passing. Homespun for sure, but nowhere near as sketchy as the checkpoints I'd come up against in Nigeria and elsewhere. The guys manning it weren't out to hustle, but equally they didn't like the look of a lone runner out on the road after dark. I showed them my passport but it didn't satisfy them. One guy in particular was a bit of a jobsworth, a proper Checkpoint Charlie. I was clearly too unusual a sight for him to let me pass unhindered. They quizzed and questioned me in French, and although I didn't understand the language, I began to take the impression that they thought I was some kind of spy, moving undercover through the darkness in order to gather information about I don't know what.

Personally, I don't think I looked very much like a spy with my sweaty running gear and my big orange beard. I was hardly dressed to slip under the radar or blend in. No matter. The guy made me sit and wait at the checkpoint for ages. I tried to ask him what was going on, why I was being detained. No answer until, eventually, a banged-up four-by-four that acted as a squad car rolled up. The guys in the squad car asked to see my passport. I showed it to them, and they all started arguing with the jobsworth. I gleaned from the argument that they were annoyed at having been called out over a nothing issue like this, a British tourist with every right to be on the road at night. The jobsworth stood firm. I was packed into the squad car and taken to a police station 20 minutes away and, yet again, made to wait.

There had been times over the past few months when this turn of events would have worried me. Not now. I could tell that the officers at the police station were peeved with the whole affair. When

I sat down with the head guy, and he asked me who I was and what I was doing, I was able to show him articles on the internet that backed up my story. He read them with one raised eyebrow, then gave me a slightly patronising smile like I was a kid who'd just scored in a school football match. He let me go. My time as a suspected spy was quickly over. The police drove me back to the hotel where the boys were staying, and the next morning I started my run at the checkpoint. No questions asked.

19

MOODY GEEZER

Motivation is fickle. It ebbs and flows. As the border of Guinea approached, my mood dropped again. I'd been on the road for 250 days and there was still much further to go. I was beginning to feel like I had nothing left in the tank, and try though I might, I couldn't ignore that I still had to run the entire Sahara Desert. Perhaps most dauntingly, the route through Guinea was mountainous. I hoped that the mountains of Cameroon and Nigeria doing me in had been a one-off, that my body was now accustomed to that kind of running and the terrain to come would not affect it in the same way. Deep down, I knew it was unlikely.

We reached the border on Christmas Eve. There had been no real signs of Christmas in Ivory Coast, although the locals were warm and encouraging as I pounded the tarmac. It didn't really bother me. I'd not celebrated Christmas for the past few years. Last year I'd been training by myself in Gran Canaria. The Christmas before that I'd seen a few mates on Christmas morning then gone for a run in the afternoon. In my head, Christmas wasn't a big deal. That's not to say, though, that it wasn't peculiar crossing the border into Guinea when I knew that Emily, and my family, would be getting ready to celebrate so many thousands of miles away.

Sometimes the thought of home hits you harder than others, and makes you realise how far away you are. We managed to celebrate Christmas Day in our own unique way on our first day in Guinea. We bought some palm wine from a lady on the side of the road, drank a few rough mouthfuls and then I ran a cheeky marathon. Guus had sourced some live roosters in Ivory Coast, which we kept with us in the car for a couple of days. We killed and plucked our short-lived travelling companions for Christmas dinner, and cooked them over a huge camp fire. Pretty banging.

The next day I continued to run under the shadow of a fairly significant hangover. Note to self: ultramarathons and palm wine don't mix. My Boxing Day run was a gruelling introduction to the country that would be perhaps my least favourite of the entire mission. I'd had the luxury of decent tarmac throughout Ghana and Ivory Coast. That luxury came to an end in Guinea, as did the luxury of internet service. In 2021, Guinea had been subject to a military coup. The new government had ordered the restriction of internet access across the country, supposedly as a security measure but in reality to prevent anti-government protestors from coordinating their activities. Guinea borders Sierra Leone and Liberia, both of which are countries with a troubled past and the origin of many displaced people in Guinea. The infrastructure is terrible, and while I didn't feel that this country was anything like as hostile as the DRC, it was certainly a lot less welcoming than Ghana or Ivory Coast. There was a nationwide shortage of fuel, which led to terrible problems both for the local economy and for us – the guys spent hours queuing to fill up the vehicles. All in all, this felt like a place where there was a good deal of unnecessary suffering.

Earlier in the mission, I'd tried to keep an open mind about the way the countries I visited were run. Who was I, a kid from Worthing, to say how people from different cultures should organise their social structures and systems of government? My approach was to learn rather than judge, and to acknowledge that there was always complexity that I couldn't see. In Guinea, though, I struggled to maintain that approach. I couldn't respect a regime that shut down the communications towers in order to silence their own people. It gave off North Korea vibes. It felt deeply wrong.

Or maybe my mood meant that I was finding it harder to see the good in places. Maybe our ability to keep an open mind relies on the state of that mind. When I told the guys how difficult I was finding Guinea as a place, they didn't quite seem to share my view. Perhaps my perspective was the problem.

We relied on Google Maps for navigation throughout the continent. In Guinea we had to download our routes in advance but here, as in most of Africa, we'd find ourselves sticking to one road for hundreds of kilometres at a time. So the lack of internet didn't prove massively debilitating in terms of navigation. Once again, though, our presence started to grab the attention of the authorities. On Day 260, we were camping near the Sierra Leone border when an army truck carrying ten armed guys pulled up in the darkness. We were out in the bush, far from the road, but they found us anyway. They weren't friendly. They clicked their guns at us and told us we couldn't camp here because of the risk of terrorism. They insisted that we accompany them to a nearby military base, a basic encampment of concrete buildings for a couple of hundred soldiers, strategically situated on the top of a hill. Basic facilities. The toilet was a shed with a hole in the ground. For our own safety we slept in the van within the confines of the military base, and no doubt the soldiers had a point. This was a sketchy neighbourhood. We didn't see any violence, but that didn't mean it didn't exist.

And then there were the mountains of Guinea. I'd been expecting them, but still: even though I'd hoped they wouldn't hurt my back, I knew they would. I had no option, though, but to cross them. They became predictably relentless, and I did everything I could to take the shortest possible route through that terrain. At one stage Guus and I took a shortcut through a mountain pass that the van couldn't manage but the four-by-four could, much as we had done when crossing from Cameroon to Nigeria. The rigours of the mission hit me hard. We'd eaten well in Ghana and Ivory Coast, but in Guinea the quality of the food had deteriorated. Omelettes that we bought on the side of the road were contaminated with sand. Grim noodles and dirty bread. We had no option but to eat this stuff, and I had no option but to consume more of it than the others because my calorie requirements were so much larger. I had to drink more water than the others too. It meant I was statistically more likely to get food poisoning, and another bout hit me in the mountains. I felt rough all day, got to the end of my run and spewed everywhere. We were on a mud track leading through jungly, mountainous terrain. Under other circumstances it would have been beautiful. Through the filter of food poisoning, it was anything but. I didn't want to stop my forward momentum, but equally I knew that if I pushed myself too hard while I was ill, it could delay me further. So for a few days I only completed half marathons while I waited for my symptoms to subside. When I felt ready to increase the mileage again, I only upped it back to 50-kilometre days. Even they were tough going.

The uncertainties of the road ahead did not help my mood. I was physically and mentally done in. The mission had been far harder on my body and my mind than I ever expected. The mountains hurt my back and the lack of internet meant I couldn't speak to Emily, which always made things worse. It made me feel more isolated somehow. I knew I still had to cross the Sahara Desert, and we still had not figured out the issue of crossing the Algerian border – an issue that threatened to be terminal to the mission. There was a strong chance that everything I'd endured would be for nothing. Our best plan – to apply for residency in Mauritania and then for a resident's visa into Algeria – struck me as being a non-starter. Our worst plan – to cross the Algerian border illegally – struck me as being a shortcut to a North African prison. Part of me respected the stubbornness of the Algerian border policy. They simply wanted to protect their land and their culture from the Western world. They had no interest in a tourist economy. They rejected outside influences. But still: my thoughts about that border crossing were, to put it mildly, demotivating. Time was running out. The lack of internet compromised our ability to research the problem. They say that action is the cure for anxiety.

I felt impotent, and a dread hung over me that a tedious logistical issue would make it all for nothing.

So as I ran, and tried to keep my mind off the mountains, and the food poisoning, and the poverty, and the lack of communication with the outside world, I schemed. When we emerged from the mountains of Guinea on New Year's Eve, I proposed to the others an idea that had been brewing over the past few days. What if we published a video online explaining that Algeria wouldn't let us in and that we needed our followers' help to get the attention of those high up in the Algerian government? What if we tried to go viral?

Guus and Stan weren't keen. Guus had been in charge of our logistics, and everybody he spoke to about this idea had reservations. They explained that Algeria was a very closed society, and that the Algerians would find this move culturally disrespectful. In highlighting their strict border control policies, we risked making them look bad. By suggesting that we were worthy of special treatment, we risked them making an example of us. And it was a zero sum game: if, having been backed into a corner, the Algerian authorities said no, we would have nowhere else to go. No other options. If we won, we'd win big. If we lost, the mission was over.

All good points. But the bottom line was that I didn't think the Mauritanian residency plan would work either. I didn't see that we had an option. We needed a bolder plan, properly executed. It was a risk, for sure, but I'd learned, over the past few months, that leadership was about making the big decisions. If my gut told me that my approach was the right one, I needed to go with it. I could live with being wrong if I'd followed my own instinct, but to be wrong having followed someone else's advice when I didn't truly believe in it would have sat badly with me. I decided that, when we entered Senegal, we would put the plan into action.

I also had another plan for the weeks ahead. We were losing money on the YouTube videos we'd been making to raise the profile of the mission. The cost of keeping Stan and Jamie on the team far outweighed our revenue. Perhaps more importantly, my mood had dipped to the point where I could no longer face having a camera in my face all day long. It felt like an unnecessary interference when I was already struggling to maintain my motivation. I decided that when we reached Mauritania, and the tarmac road ran out and I was faced with the gruelling prospect of hundreds of kilometres of loose desert sand, I would send Stan and Jamie home. I sat them down one day in Guinea to explain my reasoning. They weren't thrilled, of course, but they seemed to accept the decision. Or at least they seemed to accept that I wasn't in the right frame of mind to argue. Guinea had knocked all that out of me.

• • •

Before the border between Guinea and Senegal, there is a checkpoint. At the checkpoint, in time-honoured fashion, you're expected to pay a bribe. I was done with bribes. I decided to avoid the inevitable outstretched palm by running round the perimeter of the little village that hosted the checkpoint, and proceeding to the border post from there. I sneaked past the buildings and ran to the border, keen to put Guinea behind me. I failed to account for the fact that the guards at the checkpoint and the guards at the border were in communication with each other. When I arrived at the border post, they knew I hadn't paid the requisite bribe, and they weren't happy about it. They were hostile. They demanded money.

I was fed up with Guinea. More than that, I was fed up with the constant bribes people expected me to pay, with everyone trying to fleece us. I decided to have a bit of fun. The guy demanding payment was the head honcho of the whole border post. Did he look like a serious guy? Was he wearing an official uniform? No. He sported a T-shirt with a photograph of a pair of women's breasts printed on the front, along with the words 'Nice Boobs'. Very dignified. 'Okay,' I told him. 'I'll pay your money on one condition: we swap T-shirts.'

Guus, who was translating into French, gave me a strange look. An 'I'm not sure how this is going to turn out' kind of look. Fair enough. Either the guy would find it funny and let us through, or he'd be pissed off and they'd hold us there for ages. Whatever. Guus issued my demand. The guy, looking pretty striking in his nudie T-shirt, gave me a hard look. Then he burst out laughing. He nodded, removed his T-shirt and handed it to me. I returned the favour with a T-shirt of my own (a clean one, I should add), plus the few quid being demanded as a bribe. Suddenly the tension dissolved from the situation. They let us through and we crossed the border.

Goodbye, Guinea. Been there. Done that. Got the T-shirt.

20

VIRAL GEEZER

We entered Senegal on Day 270. I was pleased to have Guinea behind us, and pleased to have better tarmac under my feet. Better roads, better shops, less reliance on dodgy omelettes at the side of the road. Guus visited a French supermarket when we arrived in Senegal and returned to the van laden with boxes of crisps, sweets, milk, cheese and cake – all the goodies I'd been craving and which had been unobtainable in Guinea. He even managed to find an ice cream. Bliss! It almost distracted me from the fact that my hip flexors were spaghetti and I still had 4,000 kilometres to run.

Our route would not take us to the coastal capital of Dakar, so I couldn't compare it to the other capital cities I'd visited. The rural areas of Africa are significantly different to the capitals. As we headed north, however – past Gambia, whose land borders are completely surrounded by Senegal – I certainly gained the impression of a well-developed country with a much easier vibe than Guinea. Instead of motorbikes we saw donkeys, and horses with carts. Beautiful, colourful markets lined the streets. It was calmer, more tolerant of and welcoming to expats and tourists. Or perhaps that was just me, and my mood was improving. Our understanding was that Senegal had one of the best-functioning democracies in Africa. It's a mostly Islamic country, and it felt as if it had been touched by Arabic culture. We saw men in kaftans and women in hijabs, a sure sign that now we were venturing into the northern part of the continent, and so beginning the final section of the mission. We saw big, beautiful mosques and heard the call to prayer. I had the sense that religion was a strong social glue, and although I am not Muslim, I felt the distinct presence of God, whatever I and the people around me perceived Him to be. People prayed five times a day, they used the word 'Allah' frequently in their conversation. And since alcohol was forbidden, there was a far more relaxed atmosphere.

Some people might find this proximity to a religious culture to be suffocating. I found it a comfort. It appealed to me that the whole community seemed focused, to some extent, on spiritual matters. It resonated, echoing the focus I achieved when running. The run through Senegal was one of my favourite stretches. I was among a community that had put in place structures that enabled them to focus on the spiritual. In some ways, I had done the same.

In Senegal, we put into action my Algerian plan. I posted a video asking for anyone and everyone who might have any influence to help us with our Algerian visas. It was a cry for help, and my hope was that we'd receive an immediate response. The video went viral. Millions of people watched it. Thousands commented and messaged and shared. News stations picked it up. Within a couple of days, a bunch of British politicians were on the case, lobbying all their contacts in Algeria. Andrew Mitchell, who held the post of Minister of State for Development and Africa, got behind us. Likewise my local MP, Tim Loughton. Alastair Campbell, Tony Blair's former press secretary, made contact. It felt pretty mad to know that a guy who had sat in the same room as prime ministers and presidents was interested in our mission.

But then, a blow. The government agency that monitors and advises on the safety of foreign travel for UK citizens told me that the region to which I wanted to travel was too dangerous. They couldn't help me in my attempts because, if they did so, and something went wrong, it would undermine their whole system. It didn't matter how widely my video was distributed; nothing could officially be done from the UK end. That option was closed.

Maybe the guys had been right. Maybe I'd made a bad call. Maybe this was the end of the mission.

Except, by now my plight was the subject of UK news broadcasts, and then it was the subject of Algerian news broadcasts. And behind the scenes, British officials approached Algerian officials, and the bush telegraph did its thing, and conversations were had, and suddenly the story came to the attention of high-up geezers in the Algerian government, just as I'd hoped it would. Would they take offence? Would they think I was backing them into a corner?

Five days after I'd initially published my video, I received a tweet from the Algerian embassy in the UK. It said that I could obtain a visa from any Algerian embassy in West Africa. An email followed, explaining that President Tebboune of Algeria had personally approved the visa.

Which I thought was pretty gangster.

I wasn't the only person who thought that. Elon Musk, owner of X (formerly Twitter), tweeted to say that this was the best of the platform. I couldn't help but think about how far we'd come. A few months ago, when we'd started out in South Africa, barely anybody knew about our mission. I didn't know if I'd be able to drum up enough interest to raise the funds to complete it. Now I was receiving tweets from presidents and the world's richest and most influential people.

That moment marked an uptick in my mood. Perhaps I hadn't realised how heavily the Algerian problem had been weighing on me, or how anxious I'd felt at the prospect that everything I'd endured would have been for nothing. Now, there were no more big administrative issues to thwart our plans. Sure, I still had the entire Sahara Desert ahead of me, but all I had to do was focus on running.

By the time we heard the news about the Algerian visa, we were closer to Nouakchott, the capital of Mauritania, than we were to Dakar, the capital of Senegal (which in any case was not on our route). So we continued our road north to the Mauritanian border. The border crossing was straightforward, and we entered the Diawling National Park, which hosts a wide variety of bird species, as well as warthogs and wild donkeys. I wasn't there for birdwatching or donkey derbies, though. I pounded the mud path through the park, eager to reach Nouakchott and get our hands on the prized Algerian visas. The road to Nouakchott, like most in Mauritania, was sparsely populated. We passed the occasional settlement here and there where the guys could put their hands on some supplies, but no major towns.

Nouakchott itself is a desert city. Sprawling, chaotic, dirty, sandy. We rocked up to the Algerian embassy and they treated us like kings. Our visas had been approved at the very highest level, and the embassy officials took pains to treat us with a corresponding level of respect. The Algerian ambassador himself turned out, and he presented me with a book about Algeria as a gift. After all the worries we'd had about that country, this was a moment. We were buzzing to get those visas in our hands. They were the key to the final leg of the mission. And Nouakchott itself felt like a landmark. Now, when I looked at a map of Africa and traced my progress from the very southern tip, it felt like I'd put in a fair old stomp. Sure, the Sahara Desert awaited, but I'd broken the spine of the continent and the spine of my mission. My own spine felt knackered but the end, if you squinted hard enough, was in sight.

The time had come for me to set an end date so that my friends, family and all those following me knew when to be at the northern tip of Tunisia. I did the maths and worked out that at 60 kilometres a day I would hit the finish line on 7 April, which was about two months away. I announced the finish date and then the inevitable food poisoning struck again, a particularly bad bout. I was puking and shitting everywhere. I couldn't even sit up in bed. Running ultramarathons would have been a no-no under the best of conditions with this in my system. Running ultramarathons in the desert? Forget it. There was no way I could forge out into the Sahara until the illness had subsided, so I took a two-day hiatus. It meant I had to do my sums again, and up my average mileage for the final push.

Even so, my mood continued to improve. My little brother came out to visit. He was the first family I'd seen since I left the UK. To celebrate his arrival, we went for a run – a cheeky 40 kilometres that ended up with him lying on the side of the road without water or phone battery. Sorry, mate. It was good to see family, though. It was a taste of the homecoming that awaited me. I'd set out to run the entire length of Africa, and I'd nearly done it. Now all I wanted was to be back home.

But first, the desert.

21

SANDY
GEEZER

The Sahara. The largest hot desert in the world. It covers an area of more than 9 million square kilometres, spans from the Atlantic in the west to the Red Sea in the east and covers most of North Africa. A vast, arid wasteland, inhospitable not only to human life, but to any life.

I'd tried to put the Sahara to the back of mind. I knew it was going to be hard, but also knew that worrying about the difficulty of crossing it would do me no favours. There had been plenty of other hurdles to overcome on the way. My attention was best focused on those, rather than on the gruelling, desolate terrain that awaited me. As we'd headed towards Nouakchott, and the conditions had turned noticeably drier and hotter, it became impossible not to think about the trial ahead. Impossible not to think about the brutal direct sun, the lack of roads, the entire absence of infrastructure or resources. If you fly over Mauritania at night and look out of your aeroplane window, you'll see the tiny lights of occasional settlements separated by hundreds of miles of nothingness. Just the sand, which I had to cross.

There was another issue too. My original plan had been to run north to south. That would have meant that I had the prevailing winds behind me. South to north, of course, meant the opposite. It meant strong headwinds, an invisible barrier pushing me back and the likelihood of running face first into sandstorms from which any sensible human would seek immediate shelter.

We loaded up with enough water and food to see us through the desert, and as soon as I ran out of Nouakchott, the vista hit me. Vast, rolling, golden sand dunes as far as I could see. A tarmac road led into the desert from the capital city. I knew it would run out in a few hundred kilometres but, to start with at least, I had something solid underfoot. My bigger problem was the heat. Running in the middle of the day through the Sahara, with no prospect of any shade, was a forbidding prospect. I decided to run at night. It would make my life a lot easier, and meant I had a much better chance of covering the required mileage.

One morning, as the sun rose, after a full night of running and 65 kilometres behind me, I hit my first sandstorm. You don't want to be caught in a Saharan sandstorm at the best of times. You certainly don't want to be running into it, exhausted from a full night's run, with no protective gear. I could barely see where I was going. Grains of sand pelted my skin and my face. I had to cover my eyes with my hands and peer out of the tiny cracks between my fingers to stop the sand blinding me and causing permanent damage. It mitigated the impact a little, but my eyes still hurt as I struggled through the storm.

That was my first sandstorm. It was by no means my last. For a period they became an almost daily occurrence and would last for several hours at a time. They varied in intensity. Sometimes I could see ten metres ahead of me. Sometimes I could barely see two. In Ghana, Guus had bought a pair of swimming goggles because he fancied a dip in a lake. After a few days, and in the absence of any other eye protection, I decided to wear these. They were tight and hot and uncomfortable, but at least they shielded my eyeballs. The sandstorms remained a trial, however. My hair became thick with sand. Wicked, weeping sores covered my nose where the grains hit my face. I had sand in my ears. Sand in my lungs. I developed a barking, hacking cough from breathing it in.

Man, I hated those sandstorms.

Running at night was much cooler than running in the daytime. But it came with its own set of problems. I'd sleep during the day and wake up when it was dark. I'd run in the dark. I'd go to bed in the dark. I saw no sunlight for days on end. A lack of sunlight has a dramatic effect on the body and the mind. It made me miserable and, as I knew well by now, my mood directly affected my motivation. I decided I couldn't carry on running at night. I would just have to deal with the daytime heat and take it on the chin. The Saharan heat was at least not humid like the heat in the jungle. It was a fierce, parching, dry heat, but the bigger issue was the sun's rays, which pelted me all day long. I do not have the complexion for relentless sun. I smeared myself in factor 50 sunscreen several times a day, but my hands still blistered horribly where the sunscreen failed to adhere.

The tarmac finally ran out in the town of Zouérat. If you look on a map, you'll see a road marked heading north of that town, but in reality there is no road. There's just desert. From time to time, a few hardy locals will venture across the sand in their trucks and their four-by-fours, heading for the northern border of Mauritania. But they find their own routes across the sands. They make their own, just as I would have to.

I'd told Stan and Jamie that they would be leaving the mission when the tarmac road ran out. When I'd made that call, my mood had been at its lowest in Guinea, and the prospect of having cameras in my face had been quite dispiriting. Now, though, as the Sahara Desert spread out ahead of me, I was finally beginning to get the sense of an ending. With only about 50 days left to go, I felt some mental relief. I knew this section of the desert would prove to be one of the biggest challenges yet, but the end was in sight and my antipathy towards the cameras lessened. On the day they were due to leave, I told Stan and Jamie that they could stay to the end, if they wanted. And they did.

Once the tarmac ran out in Mauritania, I had a thousand kilometres of sand to cross. The terrain looked identical in every direction. I soon learned that sand underfoot has different qualities. Sometimes it's loose and granular, horrible to run on because you sink into it and your feet can't get purchase. You have to work a lot harder and adjust your running technique to raise your feet higher, and this was detrimental to my already damaged hip flexors. Sometimes it's more compact, which is considerably better from a running perspective. There are rocky sections where you risk stumbling, and dried-out riverbeds that felt like slabs of stone underfoot – by far the best running surface.

We bought dodgy diesel fuel from a little settlement. It was poor-quality stuff that caused black smoke to billow from both vehicles. Despite that, the four-by-four was just about up to the job of crossing the sand. The van wasn't. We made the decision to split up again. Stan and Jamie would cover easier terrain to the west and meet up with us in the town of Tindouf in Algeria. Their journey was going to be a hazardous one, because the van started to break down again. They reached the military encampment of Ain Ben Tili, on the border with Western Sahara, where some mechanics tried to fix the van. No success. The mechanics taught Stan and Jamie a trick with the starter motor that would let them restart the engine when it failed, but it only gave them another five kilometres before the van died completely. They were stranded in the desert until a passing truck driver agreed to tow the vehicle all the way to Tindouf. It was a characteristically kind act from the locals. The people of Mauritania were welcoming and eager to help.

In the meantime, Guus and I were alone, with scant communication with the others, or indeed with the outside world. With no internet service and no villages or landmarks to help us with our bearings, we had to locate each other by means of coordinates. For communication with the outside world we relied on a satellite phone, but this only allowed us to send and receive very short text messages. Enough to let people know we were safe, but nothing else. We forged on. At times I had to walk. If there's soft sand underfoot and you're being hit by 70 miles per hour headwinds blowing thick clouds of sand in your direction, there's no running in that. I couldn't see to navigate in the sandstorms. Even without the sandstorms, one direction was indistinguishable from any other in the Sahara, at least to my unaccustomed, sand-blasted eyes. So we loaded straight-line routes into my Garmin watch, and it would tell me at a glance – as I shielded my eyes with my hands – if I strayed from that straight line. Not an easy way to navigate, especially when I ran on into the night and my maximum visibility, even with a strong head torch, was two metres.

Despite these conditions, I kept to my daily regime of at least 60 kilometres a day. I adopted a warrior mentality. In my head, the Sahara was the final boss fight at the end of the game. The final test of my resilience. I just had to endure it.

I found motivation in ticking off the remaining days in my head. Forty-nine days. Forty-eight days. Forty-seven. There was power in this small mental technique. Despite everything I had to contend with, it allowed me to put behind me the wobbles I'd experienced throughout Guinea and Senegal. Even though these were some of the harshest conditions, even though my back would still occasionally go into spasm during the night, even though my nostrils wept where the sandstorms had ripped the skin off my nose, and the dust in my lungs forced me into fits of racking coughs every morning, the knowledge that it would soon be over had a momentum of its own. With nobody around for thousands of kilometres, I would sometimes howl and bellow into the wind and the sandstorms, a raw, primal scream that somehow gave me the strength to struggle against the elements. In Guinea and Senegal, I'd been fighting myself. Now I had a different enemy: nature. The howls boosted my energy levels. They gave voice to the battle. It felt like nature didn't want to let me through, but I was determined not to let nature win and my screams were a way of letting her know.

At night, sandstorms would howl around the four-by-four, shaking it. We'd emerge in the mornings to see a landscape that resembled a different world. Like waking up on Mars. The four-by-four was thankfully robust enough to deal with the shifting sands. It could drive over anything. We would see no living thing for days on end. Occasionally I would see a bird fly overhead, but nothing more. I was particularly grateful for Guus's presence. He understood the struggle and saw it from my point of view. As I battled the thousand kilometres of sand, he anticipated my needs in terms of food and water and rest so that all I had to think about was the running. He knew when I needed to talk, and when I needed quiet. I didn't have to think about any logistics. I just had to run.

Thirty-nine days. Thirty-eight days. Thirty-seven.

My mileage dropped a little because of the conditions. It became apparent that once we hit tarmac again I would have to run in excess of 70 kilometres a day in order to hit the finish post in time. But first we had to complete the trek across the sand, and there were more potential obstacles in our way. Mauritania meets the country of Western Sahara along its northwest border. If you look on a map, you'll see that the border is made up of straight lines – that guy in an office with a ruler again – that meet each other at right angles. The final right angle, near the Algerian border, is situated in the vicinity of the small military checkpoint of Ain Ben Tili, where Jamie and Stan had stopped to try to get the van fixed. The temptation for me was to cut across the right angle, and so stray into the territory of Western Sahara. It would save 50 or 60 kilometres on the way to the Algerian border, and allow me to recalibrate my daily mileage downwards. The guys at the checkpoint shook their heads. To stray over the border into Western Sahara, even by just a few metres, was a Very Bad Idea. The complicated politics of the region meant that the Moroccan military monitored that border closely. If anybody strayed into Western Sahara from Mauritania, they were likely to be on the wrong end of a Moroccan drone-bomb strike. It was no idle threat. After leaving the checkpoint, I plotted a much smaller shortcut, closer to the corner of the right angle, which would save me perhaps 10 kilometres. There were more vehicles in this area, driving across the sand. As I approached the invisible border in the desert, some locals spotted me, drove up and warned me off. Don't risk it, they told me. You'll be bombed.

And so I took the long way round.

Thirty-six days. Thirty-five days. Thirty-four.

On Day 318, the Algerian border post came into view. I was buzzing to see it. This tiny stretch of desert had been the source of so much uncertainty and anxiety. Now here it was, and with the bulk of the Sahara behind me, it felt amazing to approach our penultimate border. Jamie and Stan had managed to get the van fixed in Tindouf and they drove back to the border to meet us, laden with cakes to treat us after our trek through the desert.

The crossing, though, was slow. As guests of the Algerian president, there was no way the Algerians would let us run the length and breadth of their country unaccompanied. For the second time in our mission, we were to be afforded a military escort. And military escorts meant delays.

Our Algerian escorts were a little more laid back than our Angolan escorts. In Angola, we were not allowed to sleep at night in the vans, but instead had to travel miles to hotels every night. The Algerians were happy to let us camp, and happy to camp with us. They seemed better organised than the Angolans, their shifts shorter and more regulated. They were certainly welcoming and friendly. At any time we'd have between two and six guys accompanying us in one or two vehicles, but they were a tiny part of a huge military presence in Algeria. We'd been told that Algeria was a dangerous place for foreigners, but I felt safe here. The protection of guys with big guns might have contributed to this.

For the first time in two weeks, we found mobile service. My phone went berserk with messages – a reminder that although we had felt isolated in the Sahara, the eyes of the world were still on us. We reached Tindouf, which felt like a former military outpost marking the Algerian border that had grown over the years into a bigger town while retaining its military flavour. Here we experienced the hospitality of the hotel where Jamie and Stan had been waiting for us. The owners had heard of our mission and treated us royally. Their hospitality was overwhelming, as was the comfort of a real bed after weeks in the Mauritanian desert. But I couldn't relax. The end date was set and I still had a couple of thousand kilometres to run. It was blissful to feel tarmac under my feet, but we were still in the Sahara. The heat remained brutal, the terrain vast and unwelcoming on either side of the road, and I couldn't get complacent. I might have 14,000 kilometres behind me, but the mission could just as easily fail in the final month as the first.

I ran a good few hundred kilometres after Tindouf before I reached the next town, maintaining a daily average of around 70 kilometres in order to hit my self-imposed deadline. I'd never run such a high mileage for such a sustained period, and my body still hurt and every step was a struggle, but there was no weasling out of it. The game's the game.

• • •

One of the valuable things about travel is that it opens your eyes to the lives of others and helps you put your own struggles into perspective. The rigours of the road were nothing compared to the hardships endured by the displaced inhabitants of a vast refugee camp we visited in the region of Tindouf. This camp hosted refugees from Western Sahara, who had been forced from their homeland because of war. Disenfranchised and living in harsh desert conditions, the displaced Saharawis have attracted the attention of volunteers and aid workers, who aim to improve the life outcomes of the refugees through arts and sports. Our visit to the camp was an eye-opening one. Had the plight of the Saharawis been that of Europeans, the world would know about it. As it was, they felt like a forgotten community, reliant on the kindness of others.

I'd been looking for an African charity with which I could share any money we raised through our fundraising attempts (along with The Running Charity in the UK), and I found it here in southern Algeria. Sandblast aims to build awareness and solidarity for the indigenous people of Western Sahara and to advocate for their UN-recognised right to self-determination. They run education programmes in the camps for young people. Having seen their work, this was a cause I could get behind.

• • •

With 20 days to go, I had nearly 1,500 kilometres to run. The Sahara Desert still surrounded us. The van continued to break down and we became reliant on the efforts of friendly Algerian mechanics. Time and efficiency became paramount. In order to cover the necessary mileage every day, we had to camp precisely where I stopped every night. There was no fat in the schedule for us to find hotels or any kind of creature comforts. I ran deep into the night, slept, and started again the moment I awoke. We hit more sandstorms. They performed their old trick of sapping my energy and morale, but I couldn't let them hinder me. I donned the old goggles once more and ploughed into the headwinds, the whole landscape a brutal cloud of razor-sharp sand. I compared it to trying to run a couple of marathons while eight strongmen attempted to hold you back, brandishing cheese graters and throwing sawdust in your eyes. When I took my breaks I was barely able to talk. Mouthfuls of sand made me spew, and I had to cover my face with cloth to keep the grit out of my lungs. The time it took me to run 70 kilometres and get eight hours' sleep was greater than 24 hours, so our daily routine became mangled and my night shifts grew longer.

Gradually, kilometre by kilometre, step by step, the desert started to fade. Nature started to give us clues that the terrain was changing. Sandstorms gave way to rain and colossal thunderstorms. Lightning cracked the sky overhead. Somehow, though, the rain failed to cleanse the air of sand, and then the sandstorms returned anyway, reminding us that we weren't quite out of the desert yet. I ran through the torrential rain and blinding sand and every kind of weather in between. The temperature fluctuated between baking heat and freezing cold. Hailstorms hit and pelted me with marbles of ice. The harsh wind bit my skin.

I couldn't stop to take shelter. Time was against me.

Sixteen days. Fifteen days. Fourteen.

Our route became more populated, but the conditions became, if anything, more treacherous. There was ice on the road, and perversely I found myself craving the heat of sub-Saharan Africa. The rainstorms became impossible to run through, and then, to our astonishment, the rain turned to snow. If I'd been asked to predict the weather during my mission, I certainly would never have imagined a snowstorm in the Algerian desert. Those conditions were so difficult that I took the decision to run just 28 kilometres on Day 339. With so few days left to run, each that I failed to make my target had a knock-on effect on my mileage for the remaining days. Having taken shelter from the snowstorm, I would have to stomp even further in the final days of the mission.

And then this thing would be done.

I had less than two weeks to go.

22

TEARFUL GEEZER

The publicity for the mission increased crazily in these final couple of weeks. My followers rocketed, the metrics went mad and donations to our charities swelled. I barely had time for any of this to register. I could do nothing but run and sleep. When, with six days to go, our military escort messed up their logistics, stopped me running after 35 kilometres and tried to escort me out of the country, before finally understanding the situation, it only made the final days more gruelling. I had to up my daily mileage to 85 kilometres, more than two marathons, more than I'd ever run on a sustained basis before. Because if I didn't, I wouldn't reach the finish line in time.

Thank goodness for the kindness of the Algerian people. If their government had seemed, at first, hostile to outsiders, the civilians were the very opposite. Word of our arrival in their country had spread, and people sought us out. They helped fix the ever-broken van. They gave us food. It was Ramadan while we were there, which meant a great deal in this Muslim land. The people would fast all day, but at the evening call to prayer they would feast. Their traditions appealed to me. I liked the way the community came together in their acts of sacrifice and celebration.

There was no room in my mind or schedule, though, for partying. I didn't delude myself about the difficulty of running 85 kilometres a day for the final few days. With the desert behind us, the terrain turned green and lush. No matter: the running was still pure grind. Even now, with the finish line so close, there was every possibility that my body would give out on me. That the sheer magnitude of the effort would become too much. The distance of the run had increased from 15,000 to nearly 16,000 kilometres because of all the delays and detours. Running 85 kilometres a day doesn't become easier when you have 16,000 kilometres behind you, however. It becomes harder. I couldn't be complacent. I couldn't relax. The people around me could celebrate as much as they wanted. I just had to run.

These were busy days for the team too. The finish line was an important moment in terms of content and logistics. We'd planned a party at the end and the guys had plenty to do to ensure everything went smoothly. There was no time for us to sit around the campfire and reflect about the highs and lows of the mission, or the lessons we'd learned. We were all focused on our jobs. We all had our hands full.

Six days. Five days. Four.

. . .

Our final border crossing, into Tunisia, took place late at night after another 85-kilometre stomp. A straightforward crossing. Tunisia was visa-free for us, and we were expected. We said goodbye to our Algerian military escort and entered our sixteenth

African country. The country that, at times, I'd wondered if we'd ever reach. Another military escort awaited me here, to accompany me to the finish line.

And it started to feel real. I knew that my mum and dad would be coming out to see me at the finish line, along with both my brothers, my oldest mates from school and, of course, Emily. We hadn't seen each other for a year, but our almost daily conversations across the thousands of miles had brought us ever closer. The prospect of seeing her kept me moving.

And I needed motivation. My path through Tunisia meant some crazy elevation. Not ideal when your back's a mess and you're running a double marathon every day.

Three days. Two days.

One.

And with a day to go, it suddenly struck me how much bigger this thing had become than I had expected. I'd put it out on my social media channels that anybody who wanted to run the final stretch with me could do so, and far more people were making the journey out to Tunisia than I expected. The media coverage was insane. I tried not to think about it too much. I'd started this mission nearly a year previously for no reason other than to challenge myself. I wasn't here for the publicity. The limelight felt uncomfortable. I didn't know how I would feel, seeing all these people and knowing that they were there for me. I'd thought about finishing for so long, and was excited to do so. But having endured so much, I couldn't predict what my reaction would be, or how I'd deal with that moment. Was I the same person who had set out in South Africa? Had the intervening 16,000 kilometres changed me?

I started the day in tears as I set out from camp for the final time, leaving the boys to follow me. Those tears came and went throughout that day. At a petrol station that marked the start of the last marathon of the mission, a crowd awaited me. There were faces I recognised and faces I didn't. There were cameras and there was chaos. There were babies and guys in Hardest Geezer beards. They cheered as I came into view, and it took everything I had to hold my emotions in.

We ran together, a crazy, joyful crowd of marathon runners, a convoy of cars and vans and bikes. All the feels, boys and girls. All the feels.

And there were plenty more feels to come. I was 30 kilometres from the finish line when, among the supporters lining the road ahead, I saw two figures. The first figure was my younger brother. He ran towards me. And behind him was the second figure. My dad. He put his arms around me. I put my arms around him. We cried. As we held each other and wept, I couldn't help but think of all that had happened in the past. Of my fractured relationship with my parents. Of the moment when, stuck on the back of a tiny motorbike deep in the jungle of the DRC, I had doubted that this moment would ever come. Of the fear that I was going to die, of never being able to hug my loved ones again. My dad couldn't believe how many people had come out to see me finish. He couldn't believe how many people had told him that watching me run the entire length of Africa had helped them in some way. He said that he was proud of me. I'll never forget that. It meant so much. Those few words, perhaps more than anything else, made the whole mission worthwhile. I realised in that moment how much I admired him. He'd suffered from ill mental health in the past, but was in a much better place now, and able to talk openly about it. He'd been on his own journey, as difficult in its way as mine, if not more. I decided there and then that I would follow his example and speak openly about my own struggles, some of which you have now read about in this book. We ran, arm in arm, for a couple of kilometres. I'd run 16,000 of them, but those couple of kilometres will stick in my mind for as long as I live.

Hundreds of people joined me for the final kilometres. Strangers and friends whom we'd met along the road. Guus, Stan and Jamie were with me, of course. But I'd also flown out the other guys who'd been such an integral part of the mission: Harry, Jarred and James. I so appreciated their presence, and the presence of everybody who ran with me. There is strength in community, and after so many thousands of kilometres of solitary running, I realised there is strength in companionship. I felt powerful with so many people around me. Like I was leading a charge through the beautiful, green Tunisian countryside, with the blue sky overhead. And as I crested the final hill and saw the Mediterranean shimmering in the distance, I cried again. That day was a series of moments of realisation that everything I'd worked for had paid off. The pain and the relentless grind was all going to stop, and I could say: I'd done it.

• • •

Ras Angela. The most northerly point of the continent. They'd set up a ribbon at the finish line and the crowd that surrounded it was like nothing I could have imagined. Friends and family and supporters and the world's media were there, and a roar erupted as my convoy of runners and I approached. With the entire continent behind me, I breached the ribbon, arms aloft. And so many people cheered and crowded around, and so surreal was the moment, that I could hardly identify anyone. A sea of faces. A haze, made hazier by the relief and the exhaustion and the elation. But one face shone clearly in the crowd. One face did not merge with all the others. It was the face I'd kept in my mind every day for the past year, whose voice had sustained me through the long, lonely hours on the road. Emily was so beautiful. Like an angel. I ran to her and gave her a big cuddle and for a few seconds it was just the two of us, together again, at last. And we cried, and suddenly I was able to turn and take it all in.

There were cameras everywhere, of course. A media frenzy. But I was more intent on picking out another face in the crowd. I saw my mum. Like my dad, she was in tears. I gave her a big hug. It was so brilliant to see her. She had endured so much for her family, for no recognition. Now the world's media was all on me, but really I wanted it to be on her, so that the sacrifices she had made could be properly acknowledged. I hoped, at least, that I'd made her proud. And she was proud, I think, but also relieved that she no longer had to worry about me. She didn't have to think of me lost in the jungle, or held up at gunpoint. She didn't have to worry about my safety or my health.

I realised that, in many ways, the past year had been a feat of endurance for my loved ones as well as for me. The tears they shed were tears of pride, but they were also tears of relief.

I walked to the very edge of the clifftop, and looked out over the ocean. I thought about the months past, but also the years past. I thought of the kid leaving home at 17. I thought of the dead-end jobs and the gambling and the lack of direction. And I thought of the path my life might have taken, if running had not arrived to save me.

A journey of a thousand miles starts with a single step. It ends with a single step too. My final act of the mission was to stride out into the ocean as the sun set over the horizon and on the journey. As I immersed myself, I thought of the little bottle of seawater that I'd collected in South Africa. It never made it back into the Med – it had got lost somewhere along the way – but that didn't matter. Had I known what the journey would entail, I doubt I would have collected that water anyway. The seawater had been a gimmick, like so many other things in our lives. The mission, on the other hand, was a fact. It was part of history, but more importantly it was part of me. Nobody could ever take that away.

EPILOGUE

Forty-eight hours after completing the mission, I was back in London. Worthing had to wait, because I had so many media commitments in the capital, and I was keen to keep raising money for The Running Charity and Sandblast, for whom we'd now raised over a million quid. I stood on the streets of London and somehow it was as if I was seeing them for the first time. Having seen the slums of South Africa and the impoverished villages of Angola and the DRC, I walked through the city wide-eyed with astonishment at the human ingenuity harnessed in building such vast constructions, and full of appreciation for the collective sacrifice and hard work that must have gone into creating such a city. For me it felt new and unusual to see these vast structures of steel, glass and concrete, when I'd seen so many African families living in tin-roof huts. I'd returned to my home country, but my homecoming almost felt like the next stage in the challenge. Yet another weird turn of events. Unexpected and slightly uncomfortable. When we travel, we learn about the places we visit, but we also learn about the places we leave behind.

When I finally made it back to Worthing, I started to feel more settled. I visited the same pub that I'd always been to with my mates. We went out for a curry. Baby steps towards a more normal existence. Life resumed its almost forgotten yet strangely familiar pattern. I experienced moments of real gratitude for everything we take for granted in this country. The ability to turn on a tap and pour drinking water. The ability to flick a switch and have light. The ability to travel easily and safely.

And yet, I found myself conflicted. For sure, the conditions we in the West take for granted would suggest that we live better lives than the majority of those on the vast continent of Africa. We have better health. We live longer. We have better education. We do not, as a rule, run past dead bodies on the side of the road. We do not expect to be robbed at gunpoint. But perhaps there are other metrics, just as important, where we score a little lower. Perhaps we are so obsessed with progress that we fail to consider matters of community and spirituality. Far more people in the West live isolated lives, whereas in Africa family and friendship create much closer-knit connections. Even as a stranger in an African village, people have time for you. By these metrics, there are countries in Africa far ahead of us. If we let go of the notion that we are too far advanced to pay attention to those parts of Africa where the people have less, perhaps we would learn something. Perhaps our own lives could be improved. Perhaps there is value in life beyond the material, but when we're surrounded by wealth and privilege, we fail to see it.

We think we have it all figured out. When we travel, though, and we broaden our horizons, we become exposed to the infinite complexity of life in all its messiness. We see that there are no easy conclusions about the state of the world. And so, having run the entire length of Africa, I have no conclusions to offer. No neatly packaged takeaways. No simple motivational mottoes. If there is a moral to the story, it is this: the more we learn, the more we realise how little we know.

Home hadn't changed, but I had. I found that I was much more comfortable, even with people whom I'd known for a very long time. Friends I'd been at school with. My family. It was nothing to do with them, of course. They had continued to live their lives as they'd always lived them. While I was on the road, they'd gone about their day-to-day in the ordinary way. It was me who had undergone a transformation. I'd endured hardships I couldn't even have imagined in advance of the mission. I'd broken pain barriers I'd never known existed. I'd been to dark psychological places and forced my way back up into the light. In doing so, I'd come to the realisation that enlightenment lies on the far side of the struggle. I felt more at peace with myself. I could hold my head up high.

And I could think to the future. The world is big and there are more missions out there. In moments of quiet, I look at the globe. There are many land masses to cross. Many mountain ranges to tackle. Many deserts to defeat. From time to time, my attention is drawn to the South Pole, and then to the North. I draw lines between the two and I find myself wondering: is it possible?

I know the answer: anything is possible with a gangster mindset and a refusal to let obstacles become immovable objects rather than temporary inconveniences. We all have challenges to overcome. Some we choose; some we don't. But the only way to break them down is to run straight into the headwinds and keep moving forwards. Step, by step, by step.

ACKNOWEDGEMENTS

There are so many people I could thank. You know who you are. But the Africa mission wouldn't have happened without my crew, so I want to give a massive shout-out to Stan, Harry, Jarred, Nessi, Jamie, James and Guus.

Thanks to Steven Bartlett for keeping the show on the road.

Thanks to everyone at Ebury, especially Charlotte Hardman, Jasmin Kaur, Jess Anderson, Patsy O'Neill and Jaini Haria, for believing in my story.

Thanks to Adam Parfitt for helping me find the words.

And finally, thanks to Emily for your unwavering love and support, which kept me sane throughout the Africa mission and continues to do so every day.